ACA Common Core ELA Teacher's Manual
Grades 1 - 4

for

Aesop's Childhood Adventures Series

Vincent A. Mastro
illustrations by: Anita Wells

©2013 Vangelo Media

ACA Common Core ELA Teacher's Manual
Grades 1-4
for Aesop's 1st & 2nd Books of Childhood Adventures

Copyright © 2013 by Vincent A. Mastro. All rights reserved.

Except as permitted under the United States Copyright Act, no part of this publication may be reproduced or distributed in any form or by any means, or stored in a database retrieval system, without prior written permission of the publisher.

First published 2013 by *Vangelo Media*
Special discounts are available on quantity purchases. For details, send inquiries to info@vangelomedia.com or visit www.vangelomedia.com.

Printed in the United States of America

Publisher's Cataloging-in-Publication data

Mastro, Vincent.
   ACA Common Core ELA Teacher's Manual: Grades 1-4 for Aesop's 1st and 2nd books of childhood adventures / Vincent A. Mastro.
   p. cm.
   ISBN: 978-1-940604-28-2
Audience: educators.
Summary: Pedagogical guidance on applying the Common Core standards to the stories of Aesop's Childhood Adventures series books 1 and 2.
Contents: Common core standard (RL.2, RL.3, RI.2, RI.3, W.1, W.2, W.3, W.4), common core mapping to the following stories: The tortoise and the hare, The friends and the bear, The crow and the pitcher. The goose that laid golden eggs, Three equal shares and The oak and the grass.

1. xxx
2. Aesop's fables—Adaptations. [1. Fables. 2. Folklore.] I. Aesop. II. Title.

Table of Contents

Introduction   5

Common Core Mapping Summary   6

The Tortoise and the Hare   9
   Story   10
   Reading Standards for Literature - Grades 2 & 3   21
   Reading Standards for Informational Text - Grades 2 & 3   26
   Writing - Grades 1 - 4   32
   Worksheets   35

The Friends and the Bear   53
   Story   54
   Reading Standards for Literature - Grades 2 & 3   63
   Reading Standards for Informational Text - Grades 2 & 3   67
   Writing - Grades 1 - 4   71

The Crow and the Pitcher   74
   Story   75
   Reading Standards for Literature - Grades 2 & 3   84
   Reading Standards for Informational Text - Grades 2 & 3   88
   Writing - Grade 1 - 4   93
   Worksheets   96

Introduction

This teacher's manual provides pedagogical guidance on applying the Common Core, ELA standards to *The Tortoise and the Hare, The Friends and the Bear,* and *The Crow and the Pitcher* stories of Aesop's Childhood Adventures Series. The purpose is to facilitate the teacher's efforts to create practical lesson plans. This guidance is provided in the form of tables that contain both the core standard and the guidance as illustrated below:

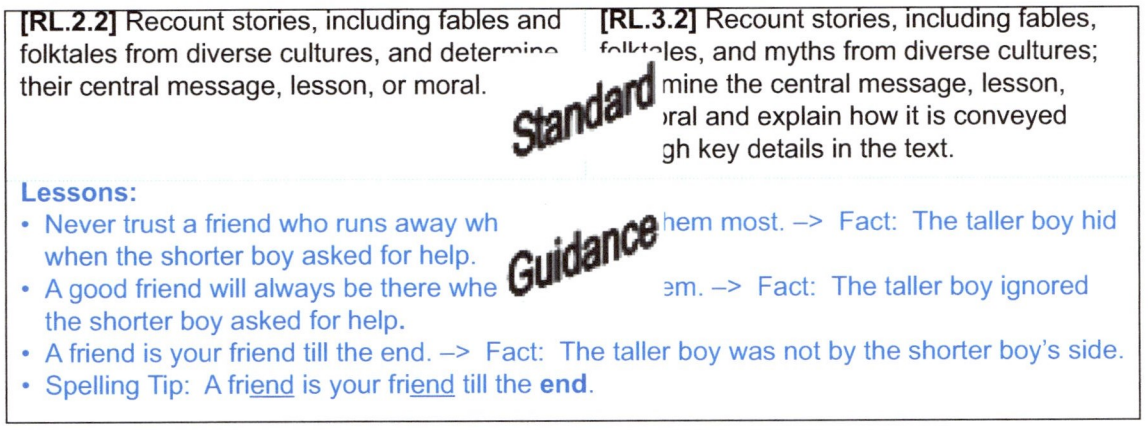

This manual also includes the pages of all 3 stories and worksheets for *The Tortoise and the Hare* and *The Crow and the Pitcher*.

The guide is organized by story and the guidance is specific to each story. However, the teacher may want to expand the scope of the compare, contrast and opinion pieces to include multiple stories.

Spiral bound: The print version of this guide was formatted so that it could be spiral bound. Any printer (such as Kinko's) can do this for a reasonable fee. They will cut the binding, punch the holes and add the spiral binding.

We are always looking for comments, fixes, updates and enhancement. Please contact us at anytime with your suggestions at: info@vangelomedia.com or go to the contact page of our website: www.vangelomedia.com.

Common Core Mapping
Summary

Common Core Standard Reading Literature		Tortoise Hare	Friends Bear	Crow Pitcher	Goose Egg	Equal Shares	Oak Grass
Grade 2	CCSS.ELA-Literacy.RL.2.1	WS	X	X	X	X	X
	CCSS.ELA-Literacy.RL.2.2	X	X	X	X	X	X
	CCSS.ELA-Literacy.RL.2.3	WS	X	X	X	X	X
	CCSS.ELA-Literacy.RL.2.4	X	X	X	X	X	X
	CCSS.ELA-Literacy.RL.2.5	X	X	X	X	X	X
	CCSS.ELA-Literacy.RL.2.6	X	X	X	X	X	X
	CCSS.ELA-Literacy.RL.2.7	WS	X	X	X	X	X
	CCSS.ELA-Literacy.RL.2.9	X	X	X	X	X	X
Grade 3	CCSS.ELA-Literacy.RL.3.1	WS	X	X	X	X	X
	CCSS.ELA-Literacy.RL.3.2	X	X	X	X	X	X
	CCSS.ELA-Literacy.RL.3.3	WS	X	X	X	X	X
	CCSS.ELA-Literacy.RL.3.4	X	X	X	X	X	X
	CCSS.ELA-Literacy.RL.3.5	X	X	X	X	X	X
	CCSS.ELA-Literacy.RL.3.6	WS	X	X	X	X	X
	CCSS.ELA-Literacy.RL.3.7	WS	X	X	X	X	X
	CCSS.ELA-Literacy.RL.3.9	X	X	X	X	X	X

NOTE: WS = Worksheet Available and guidance available in the Teacher's guide
       X = Guidance available in the Teacher's guide

Common Core Standard Reading Informational Text	Tortoise Hare	Friends Bear	Crow Pitcher	Goose Egg	Equal Shares	Oak Grass
Grade 2 CCSS.ELA-Literacy.RI.2.1	WS	X	WS	X	X	X
CCSS.ELA-Literacy.RI.2.2	WS	X	WS	X	X	X
CCSS.ELA-Literacy.RI.2.3	WS		X			
CCSS.ELA-Literacy.RI.2.4	WS	X	WS	X	X	X
CCSS.ELA-Literacy.RI.2.5	WS	X	WS			
CCSS.ELA-Literacy.RI.2.6	WS	X	WS	X	X	X
CCSS.ELA-Literacy.RI.2.7	WS	X	WS			
CCSS.ELA-Literacy.RI.2.9	X	X	X	X	X	X
Grade 3 CCSS.ELA-Literacy.RI.3.1	WS	X	WS	X	X	X
CCSS.ELA-Literacy.RI.3.2	WS	X	WS	X	X	X
CCSS.ELA-Literacy.RI.3.3	WS		WS			
CCSS.ELA-Literacy.RI.3.4	WS	X	WS	X	X	X
CCSS.ELA-Literacy.RI.3.6	X	X	X	X	X	X
CCSS.ELA-Literacy.RI.3.7	X	X	X			
CCSS.ELA-Literacy.RI.3.9	X	X	X	X	X	X

Common Core Standard Mathematics: Measurement & Data	Tortoise Hare	Friends Bear	Crow Pitcher	Goose Egg	Equal Shares	Oak Grass
Grade 2 CCSS.Math.Content.2.MD.A.1	WS					
CCSS.Math.Content.2.MD.A.2	WS					
CCSS.Math.Content.2.MD.A.3	WS					
CCSS.Math.Content.2.MD.A.4	WS					
CCSS.Math.Content.2.MD.D.9	X					
Grade 3 CCSS.Math.Content.3.MD.A.2			WS			

NOTE: WS = Worksheet Available and guidance available in the Teacher's guide

X = Guidance available in the Teacher's guide

Common Core Standard Writing		Tortoise Hare	Friends Bear	Crow Pitcher	Goose Egg	Equal Shares	Oak Grass
Grade 1	CCSS.ELA-Literacy.W.1.1	WS	X	WS	X	X	X
	CCSS.ELA-Literacy.W.1.2	WS	X	WS	X	X	X
	CCSS.ELA-Literacy.W.1.3	WS	X	WS	X	X	X
	CCSS.ELA-Literacy.W.1.5	X	X	X	X	X	X
	CCSS.ELA-Literacy.W.1.6	X	X	X	X	X	X
	CCSS.ELA-Literacy.W.1.8	X	X	X	X	X	X
Grade 2	CCSS.ELA-Literacy.W.2.1	WS	X	WS	X	X	X
	CCSS.ELA-Literacy.W.2.2	WS	X	WS	X	X	X
	CCSS.ELA-Literacy.W.2.3	WS	X	WS	X	X	X
	CCSS.ELA-Literacy.W.2.5	X	X	X	X	X	X
	CCSS.ELA-Literacy.W.2.6	X	X	X	X	X	X
	CCSS.ELA-Literacy.W.2.8	X	X	X	X	X	X
Grade 3	CCSS.ELA-Literacy.W.3.1	WS	X	WS	X	X	X
Grade 4	CCSS.ELA-Literacy.W.4.1	WS	X	WS	X	X	X

NOTE: **WS = Worksheet Available and guidance available in the Teacher's guide**
        X = Guidance available in the Teacher's guide

The Tortoise and the Hare

Common Core Mapping

The Tortoise and the Hare

"But why Nana, why?" asked Aesop.

With a big smile and a sparkle in her eye, the older one said, "Aesop, I don't know the answer to every question. Sometimes, you have to go and find the answer for yourself."

"I will, Nana. Today is the day I will find out why."

Little Aesop looked up at his grandmother. He jumped

out of her lap and on to the floor. He ran through the den, down the hall and out the door.

It was a beautiful sunny day, perfect weather for Little Aesop to go out and play.

Soon, Little Aesop came upon his friends the hare, the fox, the two mice, and the tortoise.

"Hi everyone," said Aesop.

The hare turned to Aesop and said, "I was just saying that I can run so fast that I can beat anyone in a race."

The tortoise shook her head sadly and asked, "Why do you need to brag so much?"

"It is not bragging when it is true," said the hare.

The other animals looked at each other and said nothing.

The hare turned toward the tortoise and laughed at her. "Look how short your legs are. You must be the slowest of us all!"

Aesop was disappointed in the hare for being so rude.

The tortoise replied, "I may be slow and have short legs, but I have something that you do not have."

The hare chuckled and said, "That is right, Tortoise. You do have something that none of us have. You have a big heavy shell to slow you down."

"There you go boasting again," said the tortoise.

"Do you think you can beat me in a race?"

The hare burst into laughter, as did all the other animals, except for Aesop. Aesop was worried that the tortoise would lose the race. He did not want her to be sad and he knew the hare would never stop bragging if he won.

"Is that a joke?" asked the hare. "I could dance the whole way and still beat someone as slow as you."

The mouse jumped up and down with excitement and yelled, "A race, a race! I'm going to get my checkered flag."

When the mouse returned he stood by the tree and said, "The race will start here. You will run past the big boulder, and go down the hill. Then you will run around the clover field and back up the hill to this tree. The first one to the finish line wins the race."

The tortoise was ready at the starting line, while the hare was gibbering and jabbering with all the other animals.

Aesop was worried that the race was much too long for the tortoise. He did not want her to lose.

"On your mark … get set … GO!" yelled the mouse.

The tortoise pushed herself forward, taking one slow step at a time. She was moving as fast as her little legs could

take her, but she did not get very far. All the other animals pointed at her and laughed, except for Aesop.

The hare was laughing too. They laughed until their bellies ached.

The mouse saw that the hare had not yet started the race so he yelled, "Go hare, go!"

Swoosh!

The hare took off like a dart. He ran past the tortoise, by the boulder, then down the hill, and was out of sight.

The tortoise had not gone very far at all. She had not even reached the big boulder. One of the animals yelled, "You should just give up, Tortoise. There is no way you are going to win. You are much too slow."

Aesop called out to the tortoise, "Go, Tortoise, go! You can do it!"

The tortoise looked over and smiled at Aesop and said, "I will never give up. I have something that the hare does not have." But no one understood what the tortoise was talking about.

Aesop and all the other animals ran to the top of the hill to see how far the hare had gone. To everyone's surprise, the hare was lying down next to a stump playing with the clover.

The hare saw the animals and yelled, "Look at all this clover. I am going to find one with four leaves."

After a while, the hare got bored looking for a four leaf clover and he fell asleep.

Aesop could not believe that the hare had fallen asleep during the middle of a race. It was at that moment, that Aesop understood what the tortoise meant when she had said, that she had something that the hare did not have.

Aesop smiled and walked to the finish line because he now knew, the tortoise would win the race.

Meanwhile, the tortoise just plodded on, taking one slow step at a time, focusing only on the finish line. Eventually, the tortoise passed the sleeping hare, who was snoring as he napped in the clover. She continued slowly on her way.

When the hare woke up from his nap, he saw that the tortoise was just about to cross the finish line. He leapt up, and ran as fast as he could.

But he was too late. The tortoise had crossed the finish line first and won the race!

"Congratulations!" said the fox. "It looks like slow and steady wins the race."

"That is right," replied the tortoise. "I have perseverance."

"What is perseverance?" asked the fox.

Aesop knew that the tortoise won the race because she had focused only on the race and did not give up.

Little Aesop could not wait to go home and tell his Nana about perseverance. He said good bye to his friends and headed home.

"I'm happy to see you my little one," said Aesop's grandmother, who was sitting in the den. "Did you find what you were looking for? Did you get the answer to your questions?"

"No," said Aesop as he climbed into his grandmother's lap, "I still do not know why, but I did learn that slow and steady can win a race, and I don't like it when people boast."

"That is very good Aesop, tell me more."

"Well, I saw a race today, Nana, where the tortoise beat the hare…"

When Aesop was finished telling his grandmother everything that happened, she looked at the young one with a big smile and a sparkle in her eye and said, "It sounds like you had a great adventure today. I know you did not find what you were looking for, but you did learn that bragging can hurt people and anything is possible with perseverance."

She then hugged Aesop and said, "Don't worry about your questions, Aesop. Eventually, you will find the answers to all of them because you have perseverance too."

The Tortoise and the Hare   Common Core Mapping   Reading Standards for Literature

Grade 2	Grade 3
Key Ideas and details	

[RL.2.1] Ask and answer such questions as who, what, where, when, why, and how to demonstrate understanding of key details in a text.
 	
Who:
  Nana (f): Aesop's Grandmother.
  Aesop or Little Aesop (m): Protagonist. A young boy raccoon in the why stage of life who experience the fable as it unfolds.
  Hare (m): Aesop's friend who lost the race. He boasted and was rude. He ran fast but fell asleep.
  Fox: Aesop's friend who wanted to learn the meaning of perseverance.
  Mouse (m): Aesop's friend with the checkered flag.
  Mouse: Aesop's friend who watched the race.
  Tortoise (f): Aesop's friend who won the race and had perseverance.
What: Race between a tortoise and a hare.
Where: Clover field, race track, neighborhood.
Why: To show the hare that boasting is hurtful, she would not back down, and it takes more than speed to win a race.
How: Win the race. Plodding along and not giving up (i.e. win through perseverance).
	[RL.3.1] Ask and answer questions to demonstrate understanding of a text, referring explicitly to the text as the basis for the answers.

[RL.2.2] Recount stories, including fables and folktales from diverse cultures, and determine their central message, lesson, or moral. **Lessons:** • You don't have to be the fastest to win a race. • Anything is possible with perseverance. • People don't like it when others boast. • Bragging can hurt people.	**[RL.3.2]** Recount stories, including fables, folktales, and myths from diverse cultures; determine the central message, lesson, or moral and explain how it is conveyed through key details in the text.

[RL.2.3] Describe how characters in a story respond to major events and challenges.	[RL.3.3] Describe characters in a story (e.g., their traits, motivations, or feelings) and explain how their actions contribute to the sequence of events.
Nana: Encouraged Aesop to find answers and validated his conclusions upon return. Aesop: Went out to find answers to his questions. He watched the race and encouraged Tortoise. Aesop saw that Tortoise did not give up. Aesop was excited to go home and tell his Nana about perseverance. Hare: Boasted and bragged. Made fun of Tortoise, was over confident and fell asleep. Fox: Wanted to understand perseverance. Mouse: Was excited about watching a race. Tortoise: Worked very hard running the race and won.	See grade 2 and: Nana: Without her encouragement, Aesop would not have gone out and seen the race. Aesop: Was disappointed in the hare for being so rude. Although Aesop worried that the tortoise would lose the race he never laughed at her and always encouraged her. Aesop realized that Tortoise had perseverance because she had focused only on the race and did not give up. Hare: The boasting and bragging is a form of bullying. It also motivated Tortoise to challenge Hare to a race. Finally, the hare was over confident and fell asleep. Fox: Provided a means for the author to explain perseverance. Mouse: Managed the start and finish of the race. Tortoise: Was determined to finish the race and would not be intimidated by Hare.
Craft and Structure	
[RL.2.4] Describe how words and phrases (e.g., regular beats, alliteration, rhymes, repeated lines) supply rhythm and meaning in a story, poem, or song.	[RL.3.4] Determine the meaning of words and phrases as they are used in a text, distinguishing literal from non-literal language.
The following illustrates happiness & excitement through rhythm and speed: *"Little Aesop looked up at his grandmother. He jumped out of her lap and on to the floor. He ran through the den, down the hall and out the door.* *It was a beautiful sunny day, perfect weather for Little Aesop to go out and play."*	Non-literal: • *"I could dance the whole way and still beat someone as slow as you."* • *"The hare took off like a dart."* Literal: • *"On your mark … get set … GO!"*

The Tortoise and the Hare — Common Core Mapping — Reading Standards for Literature

[RL.2.5] Describe the overall structure of a story, including describing how the beginning introduces the story and the ending concludes the action.	**[RL.3.5]** Refer to parts of stories, dramas, and poems when writing or speaking about a text, using terms such as chapter, scene, and stanza; describe how each successive part builds on earlier sections.

Every fable in the series begins and ends the same. It starts with Aesop's grandmother encouraging him to go find answers for himself and ends with her validating his conclusions. This gives the child a comforting frame of familiarity in which each story is told. As such, the child does not need to focus on the details of the beginning and end of each fable; they only need to focus on the main content.

The life lesson / moral is stated twice as an intrinsic part of each fable. The first time it is stated is by Aesop when he states the life lesson as something he has learned that day. The second time is when his grandmother validates the message.

Stating the moral twice not only acts as a reinforcement technique but it also allows for secondary or alternative life lessons to be stated as well.

[RL.2.6] Acknowledge differences in the points of view of characters, including by speaking in a different voice for each character when reading dialogue aloud.	**[RL.3.6]** Distinguish their own point of view from that of the narrator or those of the characters.

The fable is told from Aesop's perspective. As such we know what he observes and also how he feels about events.

Integration of Knowledge and Ideas

[RL.2.7] Use information gained from the illustrations and words in a print to demonstrate understanding of its characters, setting, or plot.	**[RL.3.7]** Explain how specific aspects of a text's illustrations contribute to what is conveyed by the words in a story (e.g., create mood, emphasize aspects of a character or setting).

All illustrations of Nana are designed to convey love and support. All of the animals are black and white so that the child can fill in the colors with their imagination. There is a lady bug on the clover to provide a size comparison. There are many illustrations that were purposely not included so that the child could use their imagination. For instance, there is no picture of the clover field yet there is a picture of a clover.

The Tortoise and the Hare — Common Core Mapping — Reading Standards for Literature

[RL.2.9] Compare and contrast two or more versions of the same story (e.g., Cinderella stories) by different authors or from different cultures.

Comparison with a classic adaptation: http://www.storyit.com/Classics/Stories/tortoisehare.htm
Differences:
• Aesop is a character in the Aesop's Childhood Adventures (ACA) series while Aesop is not a character in the classic adaptation.
• Story told from the perspective of Aesop as opposed to a narrator.
• The animals that watched the race are friends.
• The meadow is full of clover and the race tack is described in the ACA story
• Perseverance is defined in ACA
• The life lessons are intrinsic to the story in ACA.
• Not many illustrations in the classic adaptation.
Similarities:
• The hare brags and laughs at Tortoise.
• The animals watched the race.
• The hare fell asleep in a meadow.
• Slow and steady wins the race is one of the lessons.

[RL.3.9] Compare and contrast the themes, settings, and plots of stories written by the same author about the same or similar characters (e.g., in books from a series).

See #5 above, each story begins and ends the same.

The theme of perseverance is an intrinsic part of every story and is illustrated by Aesop as he continues, every day to find the answers to his questions. The author believes that perseverance is a fundamental to success in life and is applicable in every conceivable area of life.

The Tortoise and the Hare   Common Core Mapping   Reading Standards for Informational Text

Grade 2	Grade 3
Key Ideas and details	
[RI.2.1] Ask and answer such questions as who, what, where, when, why, and how to demonstrate understanding of key details in a text.	**[RI.3.1]** Ask and answer questions to demonstrate understanding of a text, referring explicitly to the text as the basis for the answers.

Who:
  Nana (f): Aesop's Grandmother.
  Aesop or Little Aesop (m): Protagonist. A young boy raccoon in the why stage of life who experience the fable as it unfolds.
  Hare (m): Aesop's friend who lost the race. He boasted and was rude. He ran fast but fell asleep.
  Fox: Aesop's friend who wanted to learn the meaning of perseverance.
  Mouse (m): Aesop's friend with the checkered flag.
  Mouse: Aesop's friend who watched the race.
  Tortoise (f): Aesop's friend who won the race and had perseverance.
 What: Race between a tortoise and a hare.
 Where: Clover field, race track, neighborhood.
 Why: To show the hare that boasting is hurtful, she would not back down, and it takes more than speed to win a race.
 How: Win the race. Plodding along and not giving up (i.e. win through perseverance).	

[RI.2.2] Identify the main topic of a multi-paragraph text as well as the focus of specific paragraphs within the text.	**[RI.3.2]** Determine the main idea of a text; recount the key details and explain how they support the main idea.
Perseverance illustrated via a race between a tortoise and a hare. Here are relevant excerpts from the story. • "Aesop, I don't know the answer to every question. Sometimes, you have to go and find the answer for yourself." • "I will, Nana. Today is the day I will find out why." • The hare turned to Aesop and said, "I was just saying that I can run so fast that I can beat anyone in a race." • The tortoise replied, "I may be slow and have short legs, but I have something that you do not have." • The hare burst into laughter, as did all the other animals, except for Aesop. Aesop was worried that the tortoise would lose the race. He did not want her to be sad and he knew the hare would never stop bragging if he won. • The tortoise was ready at the starting line, while the hare was gibbering and jabbering with all the other animals. • The mouse saw that the hare had not yet started the race so he yelled, "Go hare, go!" • The tortoise looked over and smiled at Aesop and said, "I will never give up. I have something that the hare does not have." • To everyone's surprise, the hare was lying down next to a stump playing with the clover. • It was at that moment, that Aesop understood what the tortoise meant when she had said, that she had something that the hare did not have.	

- *Little Aesop could not wait to go home and tell his Nana about perseverance.*
- *… he climbed into his grandmother's lap, "I still do not know why, but I did learn that slow and steady can win a race, and I don't like it when people boast."*
- *"I know you did not find what you were looking for, but you did learn that bragging can hurt people and anything is possible with perseverance."*
- *"Don't worry about your questions, Aesop. Eventually, you will find the answers to all of them because you have perseverance."*

[RI.2.3] Describe the connection between a series of historical events, scientific ideas or concepts, or steps in technical procedures in a text.	[RI.3.3] Describe the relationship between a series of historical events, scientific ideas or concepts, or steps in technical procedures in a text, using language that pertains to time, sequence, and cause/effect.

When the mouse returned he stood by the tree and said, "The race will start here. You will run past the big boulder, and go down the hill. Then you will run around the clover field and back up the hill to this tree. The first one to the finish line wins the race."

Craft and Structure

[RI.2.4] Determine the meaning of words and phrases in a text relevant to a grade 2 topic or subject area.	[RI.3.4] Determine the meaning of general academic and domain-specific words and phrases in a text relevant to a grade 3 topic or subject area.

Each vocabulary word has no more than 3 definitions where the 1st is the preferred.

adventure
1. an exciting or very unusual experience
2. a bold, usually risky undertaking; hazardous action of uncertain outcome

boast
1. to speak with exaggeration and excessive pride, especially about oneself
2. to be proud of; a cause for pride

boulder
1. a smooth rounded mass of rock that has a diameter greater than 25cm

brag
1. to imply superiority over others by speaking with exaggeration and pride about oneself
2. an old English card game similar to poker

The Tortoise and the Hare   Common Core Mapping   Reading Standards for Informational Text

burst
1. to give sudden expression to or as if to emotion
2. to break, break open, or fly apart with sudden violence
3. to appear suddenly; become visible, audible, evident, etc., all at once

chuckle
1. to laugh softly or amusedly, usually with satisfaction

congratulations
1. to praise someone on their success or on a happy occasion
2. to communicate pleasure, approval, or praise to (a person or persons); compliment

dart
1. to move swiftly; spring or start suddenly and run swiftly
2. a small, slender missile that is pointed at one end and usually feathered at the other and is propelled by hand
3. a tapered seam of fabric for adjusting the fit of a garment

eventually
1. finally; ultimately; at some later time after a long delay

fable
1. a short tale to teach a moral lesson, often with animals or inanimate objects as characters
2. a story not founded on fact
3. legends or myths collectively

fox
1. any of several carnivores of the dog family, smaller than wolves, having a pointed, slightly upturned muzzle, erect ears, and a long, bushy tail
2. a cunning or crafty person
3. the Algonquian language of the Fox, Sauk, and Kickapoo Indians

generations
1. the term of years, roughly 30 among human beings, accepted as the average period between the birth of parents and the birth of their offspring
2. a group of individuals, most of whom are the same approximate age, having similar ideas, problems, attitudes, etc.
3. a single step in natural descent, as of human beings, animals, or plants

gibbering
1. to speak foolishly; chatter

hare
1. a large rodent like mammal having long ears, a divided upper lip, and long hind limbs adapted for leaping, as distinguished rabbits

jabbering
1. to talk or utter rapidly, indistinctly, incoherently, or nonsensically; chatter

mice
1. small animal of various rodent and marsupial families
2. a quiet, timid person
3. a device that moves the cursor on a computer screen to any position

perseverance
1. steady persistence in a course of action or purpose, especially in spite of difficulties, obstacles, or discouragement

plod
1. to walk heavily or move laboriously in a tediously slow manner
2. to proceed under the weight of a burden

rude
1. discourteous or impolite, especially in a deliberate way
2. without culture, learning, or refinement
3. rough in manners or behavior; unmannerly; uncouth

sparkle
1. to shine or glisten with little gleams of light, as a brilliant gem; glitter
2. to emit little sparks, as burning matter
3. to be brilliant, lively, or vivacious

swoosh
1. to move quickly and make a rustling, swirling, or brushing sound

tortoise
1. a land turtle that is born and lives on the ground
2. a very slow person or thing

The Tortoise and the Hare   Common Core Mapping   Reading Standards for Informational Text

[RI.2.5] Know and use various text features (e.g., captions, bold print, subheadings, glossaries, indexes, electronic menus, icons) to locate key facts or information in a text efficiently.
 	
• *"On your mark … get set … GO!" yelled the mouse.*
• *"Go hare, go!*
   Swoosh! (NOTE: *this is an onomatopoeia*)
   The hare took off like a dart.
	[RI.3.5] Use text features and search tools (e.g., key words, sidebars, hyperlinks) to locate information relevant to a given topic efficiently.
	
	`n/a

[RI.2.6] Identify the main purpose of a text, including what the author wants to answer, explain, or describe. **Lessons:** • *You don't have to be the fastest to win a race.* • *Anything is possible with perseverance.* • *People don't like it when others boast.* • *Bragging can hurt people.*	**[RI.3.6]** Distinguish their own point of view from that of the author of a text. Applicable but requires student input.
**Integration of Knowledge and Ideas**	
[RI.2.7] Explain how specific images (e.g., a diagram showing how a machine works) contribute to and clarify a text.	**[RI.3.7]** Use information gained from illustrations (e.g., maps, photographs) and the words in a text to demonstrate understanding of the text (e.g., where, when, why, and how key events occur).

Option 1: Have each student draw the racetrack based on the description in the story then compare and contrast them.
Description: *When the mouse returned he stood by the tree and said, "The race will start here. You will run past the big boulder, and go down the hill. Then you will run around the clover field and back up the hill to this tree. The first one to the finish line wins the race."*

Option 2: Point out how the illustration of a clover provides sufficient information to imagine the clover field. Also the lady bug provides a rough size comparison.

The Tortoise and the Hare — Common Core Mapping — Reading Standards for Informational Text

[RI.2.9] Compare and contrast the most important points presented by two texts on the same topic.

[RI.3.9] Compare and contrast the most important points and key details presented in two texts on the same topic.

Comparison with a classic adaptation: http://www.storyit.com/Classics/Stories/tortoisehare.htm

Differences:
- Aesop is a character in the Aesop's Childhood Adventures (ACA) series while Aesop is not a character in the classic adaptation.
- Story told from the perspective of Aesop as opposed to a narrator.
- The animals that watched the race are friends.
- The meadow is full of clover and the race tack is described in the ACA story
- Perseverance is defined in ACA
- The life lessons are intrinsic to the story in ACA.
- Not many illustrations in the classic adaptation.

Similarities:
- The hare brags and laughs at Tortoise.
- The animals watched the race.
- The hare fell asleep in a meadow.
- Slow and steady wins the race is one of the lessons.

Aesop's 1st Book of Childhood Adventures — Teacher's Guide

The Tortoise and the Hare — Common Core Mapping — Writing

Grade 1	Grade 2
Text Types and Purposes	
[W.1.1] Write opinion pieces in which they introduce the topic or name the book they are writing about, state an opinion, supply a reason for the opinion, and provide some sense of closure.	**[W.2.1]** Write opinion pieces in which they introduce the topic or book they are writing about, state an opinion, supply reasons that support the opinion, use linking words (e.g., *because*, *and*, *also*) to connect opinion and reasons, and provide a concluding statement or section.

Ask the children to think about who their favorite character is and why. Then ask them to write down the name of the story; who their favorite character is; and why that character is their favorite.
Characters:
   Nana (f): Aesop's Grandmother.
   Aesop or Little Aesop (m): Protagonist. A young boy raccoon in the why stage of life who experience the fable as it unfolds.
   Hare (m): Aesop's friend who lost the race. He boasted and was rude. He ran fast but fell asleep.
   Fox: Aesop's friend who wanted to learn the meaning of perseverance.
   Mouse (m): Aesop's friend with the checkered flag.
   Mouse: Aesop's friend who watched the race.
   Tortoise (f): Aesop's friend who won the race and had perseverance.

[W.1.2] Write informative/explanatory texts in which they name a topic, supply some facts about the topic, and provide some sense of closure.	**[W.2.2]** Write informative/explanatory texts in which they introduce a topic, use facts and definitions to develop points, and provide a concluding statement or section.

Ask the children to think about the lesson(s) they learned from the story and why it is important lesson. Then have them write about it.
Lessons:
- You don't have to be the fastest to win a race –> Fact: The tortoise is the slowest and she won the race.
- Anything is possible with perseverance –> Fact: The tortoise is the slowest and she won the race. **Perseverance:** steady persistence in a course of action or purpose, especially in spite of difficulties, obstacles, or discouragement
- People don't like it when others boast –> Fact: Aesop was disappointed in Hare for 'being so rude'.
- Bragging can hurt people –> Fact: There is no direct evidence that the tortoise was hurt but the things Hare said were hurtful.

The Tortoise and the Hare — Common Core Mapping — Writing

[W.1.3] Write narratives in which they recount two or more appropriately sequenced events, include some details regarding what happened, use temporal words to signal event order, and provide some sense of closure. Option 1: Aesop went out searching for an answer to his question. He happened upon his friends. He watched the race between Tortoise and Hare. Hare fell asleep. Tortoise won the race. He then returned to Nana's house and told her what happened. Option 2: Describe the race track *'When the mouse returned he stood by the tree and said, "The race will start here. You will run past the big boulder, and go down the hill. Then you will run around the clover field and back up the hill to this tree. The first one to the finish line wins the race."*	**[W.2.3]** Write narratives in which they recount a well-elaborated event or short sequence of events, include details to describe actions, thoughts, and feelings, use temporal words to signal event order, and provide a sense of closure. See grade 1 and: Nana: Without her encouragement, Aesop would not have gone out and seen the race. Aesop: Was worried that the tortoise would lose the race. Aesop never laughed at Tortoise and always encouraged her. Aesop realized that Tortoise had perseverance because she had focused only on the race and did not give up. Hare: The boasting and bragging is a form of bullying that motivated Tortoise to challenge Hare to a race. Finally, the hare was over confident and fell asleep. Tortoise: Was determined to finish the race and would not be intimidated by Hare.

Production and Distribution of Writing

[W.1.5] With guidance and support from adults, focus on a topic, respond to questions and suggestions from peers, and add details to strengthen writing as needed. Teacher directed.	**[W.2.5]** With guidance and support from adults and peers, focus on a topic and strengthen writing as needed by revising and editing. Teacher directed.
[W.1.6] With guidance and support from adults, use a variety of digital tools to produce and publish writing, including in collaboration with peers. Teacher directed.	**[W.2.6]** With guidance and support from adults, use a variety of digital tools to produce and publish writing, including in collaboration with peers. Teacher directed.

Research to Build and Present Knowledge

[W.1.8] With guidance and support from adults, recall information from experiences or gather information from provided sources to answer a question. Have you ever demonstrated perseverance or do you know someone who has? Describe what happened.	**[W.2.8]** Recall information from experiences or gather information from provided sources to answer a question.

The Tortoise and the Hare   Common Core Mapping   Writing

Grade 3	Grade 4
Text Types and Purposes	
[W.3.1] Write opinion pieces on topics or texts, supporting a point of view with reasons. • **[W.3.1a]** Introduce the topic or text they are writing about, state an opinion, and create an organizational structure that lists reasons. • **[W.3.1b]** Provide reasons that support the opinion. • **[W.3.1c]** Use linking words and phrases (e.g., *because*, *therefore*, *since*, *for example*) to connect opinion and reasons. • **[W.3.1d]** Provide a concluding statement or section.	**[W.4.1]** Write opinion pieces on topics or texts, supporting a point of view with reasons and information. • **W.4.1a** Introduce a topic or text clearly, state an opinion, and create an organizational structure in which related ideas are grouped to support the writer's purpose. • **[W.4.1b]** Provide reasons that are supported by facts and details. • **[W.4.1c]** Link opinion and reasons using words and phrases (e.g., f*or instance*, *in order to*, *in addition*). • **[W.4.1d]** Provide a concluding statement or section related to the opinion presented.

Option 1:
- The hare said, "*It is not bragging when it is true.*" Ask the children if the hare is correct and why. Then ask them to write an opinion piece as described above.

Option 2:
Ask the children to think about who their favorite character is and why. Then ask them to write an opinion piece as described above.
Characters:
　Nana (f): Aesop's Grandmother.
　Aesop or Little Aesop (m): Protagonist. A young boy raccoon in the why stage of life who experience the fable as it unfolds.
　Hare (m): Aesop's friend who lost the race. He boasted and was rude. He ran fast but fell asleep.
　Fox: Aesop's friend who wanted to learn the meaning of perseverance.
　Mouse (m): Aesop's friend with the checkered flag.
　Mouse: Aesop's friend who watched the race.
　Tortoise (f): Aesop's friend who won the race and had perseverance.

Common Core ELA Worksheets
for

The Tortoise and the Hare

Aesop's
1st Book of
Childhood Adventures

http://www.aesopsadventures.com/

Aesop's 1st Book of Childhood Adventures

Character Traits

Teacher's Guide

Who

Name: _____ Date: _____

Aesop's 1st Book of Childhood Adventures

Teacher's Guide

Who are the characters?

Name	Who	Where
	A nice raccoon boy who went on an adventure to find the answer to his question.	Near his Nana's cottage.
		Warm cosy cottage.

Name: _____   Date: _____

Aesop's 1st Book of Childhood Adventures

Teacher's Guide

Story Facts

What?	
When?	
Where?	
Why?	
How?	

Name: _____   Date: _____

Moral Lessons Learned

Fables are stories that teach a lesson about life. Some fables have more than one life lesson or moral.

Lesson #1:

Lesson #2:

Name: _____ Date: _____

Who did this?

Connect these

- Hare ○
- Tortoise ○
- Nana ○
- Fox ○
- Aesop ○

○ Told Aesop to find answers to his questions and discussed what he learned.

○ Went out to find answers to his questions, watched the race and encouraged Tortoise.

○ Worked very hard running the race and won.

○ Boasted and made fun of Tortoise; was over confident and fell asleep.

○ Wanted to understand perseverance.

Pick one of the characters and describe what you liked or disliked about what they did.

Name: _____ Date: _____

What does this mean?

"The hare took off like a dart."
Describe what this means:

Literal ☐ Non-literal ☐

"On your mark ... get set ... GO!"
Describe what this means:

Literal ☐ Non-literal ☐

Name: _____ Date: _____

Aesop's 1st Book of Childhood Adventures

Story Sequencing

Teacher's Guide

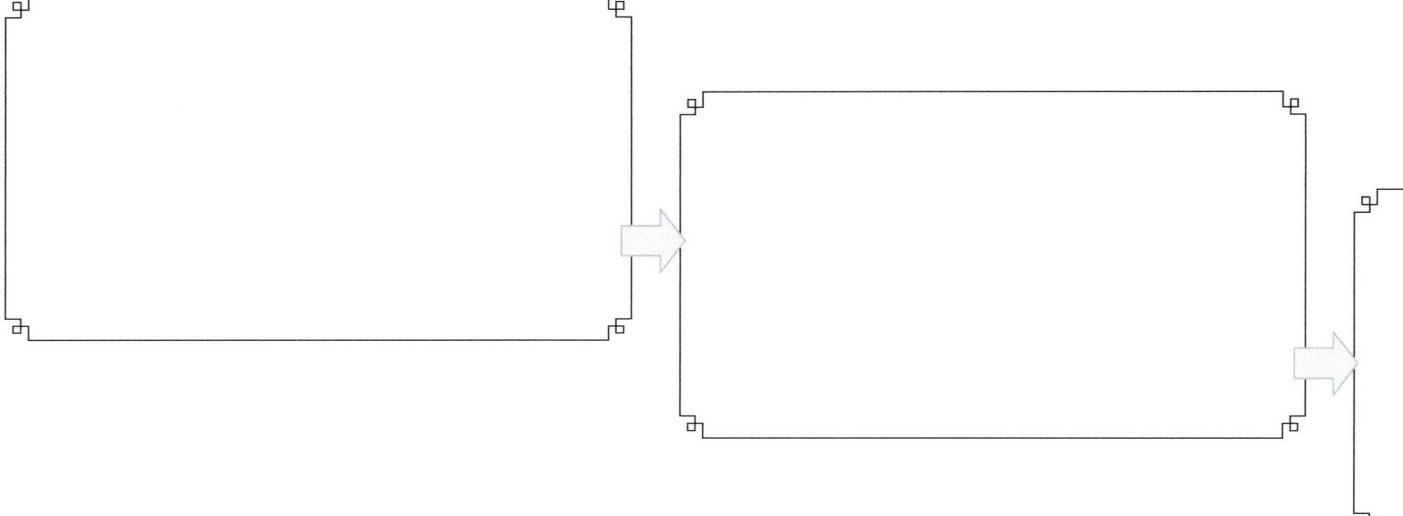

Topic: _____

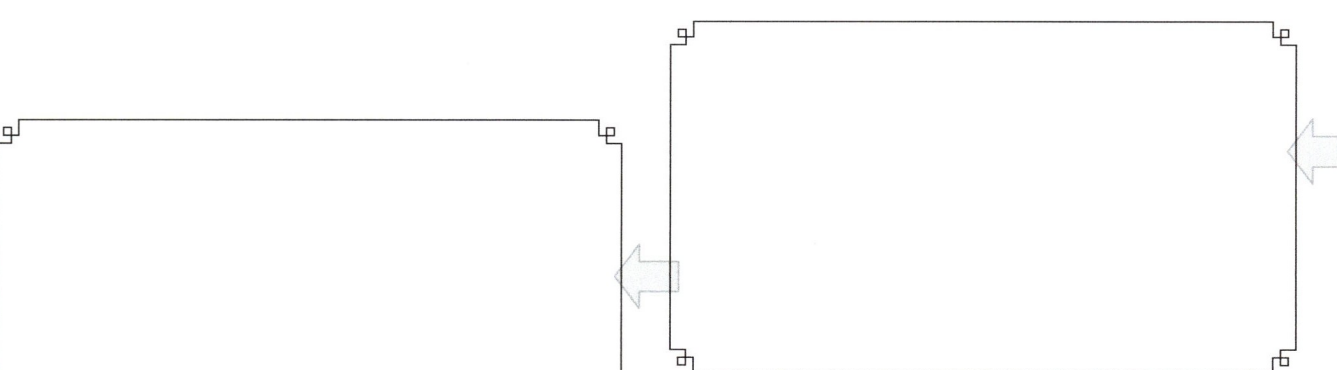

Name: _____ Date: _____

Common Core Std: RI.2.3, RI.3.3 | W.1.3, 2.3: convert this into a narrative

Story Structure

Aesop's 1st Book of Childhood Adventures — Teacher's Guide

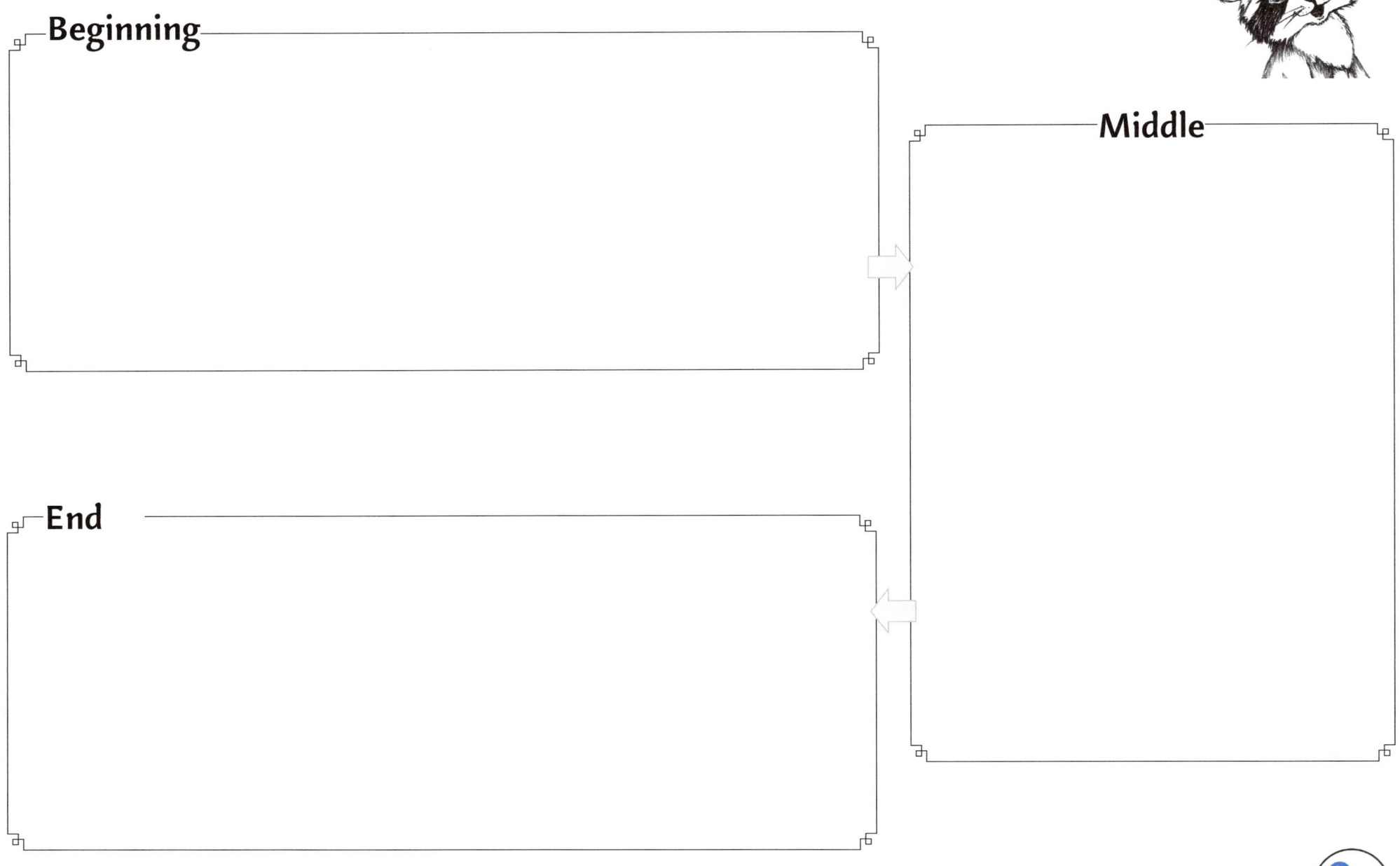

Beginning

Middle

End

Name: _____ Date: _____

Who said... ?

_____ was worried that the tortoise would lose the race.

Do you agree? _____ Why?

"It is not bragging when it is true, said _____."

Do you agree? _____ Why?

_____ was disappointed in the hare for being so rude.

Do you agree? _____ Why?

Name: _____ Date: _____

What does a clover field look like?

Name: _____ Date: _____

What does the race track look like?

"The race will start here. You will run past the big boulder, and go down the hill. Then you will run around the clover field and back up the hill to this tree. The first one to the finish line wins the race."

Name: _____ Date: _____

Vocabulary
(page 1 of 2)

adventure
An exciting or very unusual experience.
"It sounds like you had a great adventure today..."

boast
To speak with exaggeration and pride about oneself.
"There you go boasting again," said the tortoise.

boulder
A very large, smooth rock.
You will run past the big boulder, and go down the hill.

brag
To imply superiority over others by speaking with exaggeration and pride about oneself.
The tortoise shook her head sadly and asked, "Why do you need to brag so much?"

burst
To suddenly express an emotion.
The hare burst into laughter, as did all the other animals, except for Aesop.

chuckle
To laugh softly with satisfaction.
The hare chuckled and said, "That is right, Tortoise.

congratulations
To praise someone on their success or on a happy occasion.
"Congratulations!" said the fox. "It looks like slow and steady wins the race."

dart
To start suddenly and run swiftly.
The hare took off like a dart.

eventually
Finally; at some later time after a long delay.
Eventually, the tortoise passed the sleeping hare, who was snoring as he napped in the clover.

fable
A short tale to teach a moral lesson, often with animals.
Aesop's Fables

fox
A dog like animal that is smaller than wolves, having a pointed nose, erect ears, and a long, bushy tail.
Soon, Little Aesop came upon his friends the hare, the fox, the two mice, and the tortoise.

Name: _____ Date: _____

Vocabulary
(page 2 of 2)

generations
All the people born about the same time.
To my family, who taught me the importance of life lessons and the value of passing them on to future generations.

gibbering
To speak foolishly or to chatter.
The tortoise was ready at the starting line, while the hare was gibbering and jabbering with all the other animals.

hare
An animal having long ears, a divided upper lip, and long legs for jumping.
Soon, Little Aesop came upon his friends the hare, the fox, the two mice, and the tortoise.

jabbering
To talk rapidly so that no one understands.
The tortoise was ready at the starting line, while the hare was gibbering and jabbering with all the other animals.

mouse
A small animal with a long tale.
The mouse jumped up and down with excitement and yelled, "A race, a race! I'm going to get my checkered flag."

perseverance
To work steadily toward a goal while overcoming difficulties.
"That is right," replied the tortoise. "I have perseverance."

plod
To walk heavily or slowly.
Meanwhile, the tortoise just plodded on, taking one slow step at a time, focusing only on the finish line.

rude
To behave impolitely.
Aesop was disappointed in the hare for being so rude.

sparkle
To shine, glitter or glisten with little.
With a big smile and a sparkle in her eye, the older one said, "Aesop, I don't know the answer to every question...

swoosh
To move quickly and make a rustling or swirling sound.
Swoosh! The hare took off like a dart.

tortoise
A large land turtle that does not live in water.
Soon, Little Aesop came upon his friends the hare, the fox, the two mice, and the tortoise.

Name: _____ **Date:** _____

Do you agree?

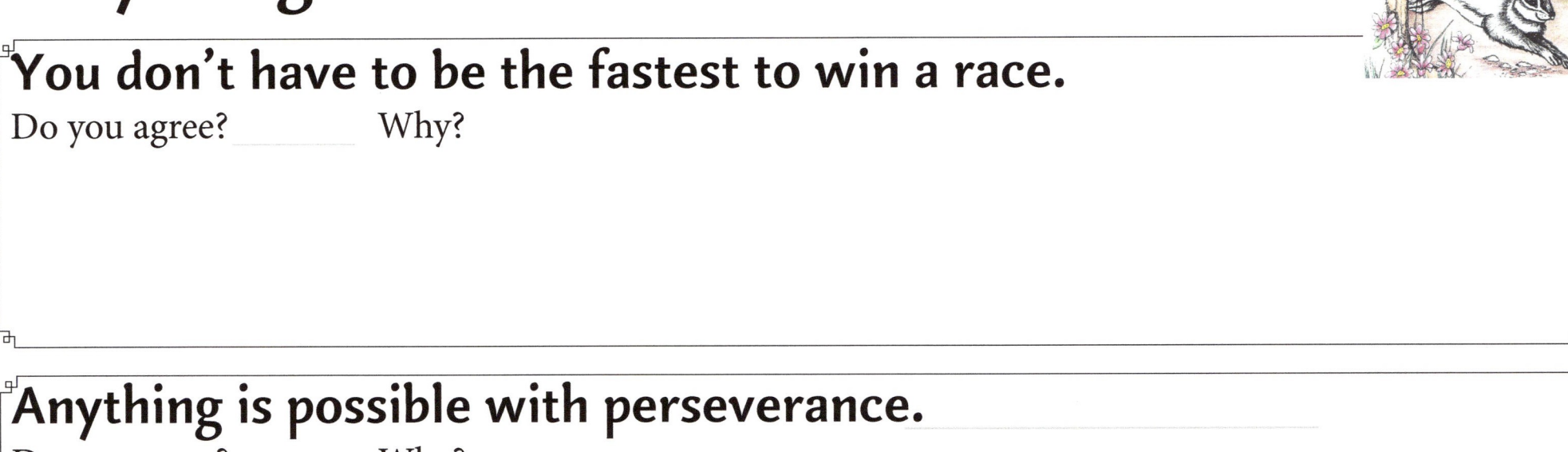

You don't have to be the fastest to win a race.
Do you agree? _____ Why?

Anything is possible with perseverance.
Do you agree? _____ Why?

Bragging can hurt people.
Do you agree? _____ Why?

Name: _____ Date: _____

Aesop's 1st Book of Childhood Adventures

Teacher's Guide

Do you agree? Why?

You don't have to be the fastest to win a race.

Name: _____   Date: _____

Aesop's 1st Book of Childhood Adventures

Teacher's Guide

Do you agree? Why?

Anything is possible with perseverance.

Name: _____ Date: _____

Common Core Standard: W.3.1, W4.1

Do you agree? Why?

Bragging can hurt people.

Name: _____ Date: _____

The Friends and the Bear

Common Core
Mapping

The Friends and the Bear

"But why Nana, why?" asked Aesop.

With a big smile and a sparkle in her eye, the older one said, "Aesop, I don't know the answer to every question. Sometimes, you have to go and find the answer for yourself."

"I will, Nana. Today is the day I will find out why."

Little Aesop looked up at his grandmother. He jumped

out of her lap and on to the floor. He ran through the den, down the hall and out the door.

It was a beautiful sunny day, perfect weather for Little Aesop to go out and play.

Soon, Little Aesop made his way deep into the forest behind his grandmother's cottage. All of a sudden he heard the sound of laughter. He poked his head around a bush and saw two boys walking toward him.

Feeling a little shy, Aesop

climbed up a tree and hid behind a branch to watch the boys.

The taller of the two boys was pulling leaves off the trees as they walked. He was teasing the shorter boy who could not reach the leaves.

Suddenly, they all heard loud rustling noises. A big, scary, brown bear rushed out from the forest on to the path in front of the boys.

Aesop was glad he was in the tree,

but he soon realized that the boys were in danger.

Aesop was frightened for the boys, and yelled to them to play dead, as his nana had taught him.

But the boys did not hear him because they did not speak raccoon. Aesop was upset and did not know what to do.

The tall boy quickly grabbed a branch and pulled himself up, into the nearest tree.

The shorter boy reached up to his friend and cried, "Pull me up! Pull me up!"

His friend ignored him and instead climbed higher and higher, up the tree where he hid among the leaves.

The shorter boy looked shocked and very scared. He threw himself down, flat upon the ground. His face was in the dirt. He did not move at all, and pretended to be dead.

The big furry brown bear shuffled over to the boy and put his muzzle to the boy's ear.

Sniff, sniff, sniff, went the bear as he stood over the frightened boy.

Aesop clung to his branch, holding his breath, frozen in fear.

The bear circled around the boy and put his muzzle to the boy's other ear.

Sniff, sniff, sniff, went the bear. He looked around and then with a low growl, walked back into the woods.

Little Aesop let out his breath with a great big whoosh. He was happy that the bear had walked away. He knew the boys would be safe, now that the bear was gone.

When the bear was out of sight, the taller boy jumped down from the tree, poked his friend and said, "Get up! Get up! The bear is gone!"

The shorter boy stood up. He was shaking and still very frightened.

"What did the bear whisper to you?"

The shorter boy paused for a moment and then said, "He told me to never trust a friend who runs away when you need them most."

Little Aesop thought for a moment about the taller boy and wondered why he had not helped his friend.

Aesop waited for the boys to leave and then he climbed down the tree and headed home.

"I'm happy to see you my little one," said Aesop's grandmother, who was sitting in the den. "Did you find what you were looking for? Did you get the answer to your questions?"

"No," said Aesop as he climbed into his grandmother's lap, "I still do not know why. But I did learn that a good friend will always be there when you need them."

"That is very good Aesop; tell me more."

"Well, I was frightened by a bear today, Nana…"

When Aesop was finished telling his grandmother everything that happened, she looked at the young one with a big smile and a sparkle in her eye and said, "It sounds like you had a great adventure today. I know you did not find what you were looking for, but you did learn about true friendship. I like to say that a friend is your friend till the end."

She then hugged Aesop and said, "Don't worry about your questions, Aesop. Eventually, you will find the answers to all of them because you have perseverance."

Aesop's 1st Book of Childhood Adventures — The Friends and the Bear — Common Core Mapping — Teacher's Guide — Reading Standards for Literature

Grade 2	Grade 3
Key Ideas and details	

[RL.2.1] Ask and answer such questions as who, what, where, when, why, and how to demonstrate understanding of key details in a text.
 	
 Who:
  Nana (f): Aesop's Grandmother.
  Aesop or Little Aesop (m): Protagonist. A young boy raccoon in the why stage of life who experience the fable as it unfolds.
  Taller boy (m): Teased the shorter boy, hid up in the tree and did not help the shorter boy.
  Shorter boy (m): To short to climb up in the tree, played dead and was almost eaten by the bear.
  Bear (m): Bear that frightened the boys, sniffed the shorter boy and almost ate him.
 What: Frightening event causes Aesop to learn about the characteristics of good friendship.
 Where: Deep in the forest behind his grandmother's cottage.
 Why: The taller boy did not demonstrate true friendship.
 How: The taller boy did not help the shorter boy when he needed him most.
	[RL.3.1] Ask and answer questions to demonstrate understanding of a text, referring explicitly to the text as the basis for the answers.

[RL.2.2] Recount stories, including fables and folktales from diverse cultures, and determine their central message, lesson, or moral. **Lessons:** • Never trust a friend who runs away when you need them most. –> Fact: The taller boy hid when the shorter boy asked for help. • A good friend will always be there when you need them. –> Fact: The taller boy ignored the shorter boy asked for help. • A friend is your friend till the end. –> Fact: The taller boy was not by the shorter boy's side. Spelling Tip: A fri**end** is your fri**end** till the **end**.	**[RL.3.2]** Recount stories, including fables, folktales, and myths from diverse cultures; determine the central message, lesson, or moral and explain how it is conveyed through key details in the text.

The Friends and the Bear — Common Core Mapping — Reading Standards for Literature

[RL.2.3] Describe how characters in a story respond to major events and challenges.	[RL.3.3] Describe characters in a story (e.g., their traits, motivations, or feelings) and explain how their actions contribute to the sequence of events.
Nana: Encouraged Aesop to find answers and validated his conclusions upon return. Aesop: Went out to find answers to his questions. He happened upon the boys walking in the forest and saw the bear come out investigate them. Aesop was frightened that the bear would eat them and he wanted to go home and tell his Nana about it. Taller boy: Teased the shorter boy, hid up in the tree, and ignored the shorter boy's pleas for help. Shorter boy: To short to climb up in the tree, played dead and was almost eaten by the bear. He also knew what is required of a good friend. Bear: Bear that frightened the boys, sniffed the shorter boy and almost ate him.	See grade 2 and: Nana: Without her encouragement, Aesop would not have gone out and seen the event. Aesop: Was afraid for himself and the boys and he was frustrated because he could not tell the boy to play dead.. Taller boy: When the bear left, the taller boy tried to make a joke of it and asked what the bear whispered to the shorter boy. Shorter boy: Knew how to play dead even though he was terrified and he also called out the taller boy when he replied that the bear told him to never trust a friend who runs away when you need them most. Bear: Just acted like a bear and lost interest in the boy because he thought he was already dead.

Craft and Structure

[RL.2.4] Describe how words and phrases (e.g., regular beats, alliteration, rhymes, repeated lines) supply rhythm and meaning in a story, poem, or song.	[RL.3.4] Determine the meaning of words and phrases as they are used in a text, distinguishing literal from non-literal language.
The following illustrates happiness & excitement through rhythm and speed: *"Little Aesop looked up at his grandmother. He jumped out of her lap and on to the floor. He ran through the den, down the hall and out the door.* *It was a beautiful sunny day, perfect weather for Little Aesop to go out and play."* *"... a friend is your friend till the end."*	Non-literal: • *"What did the bear whisper to you?"*

The Friends and the Bear — Common Core Mapping — Reading Standards for Literature

[RL.2.5] Describe the overall structure of a story, including describing how the beginning introduces the story and the ending concludes the action.	**[RL.3.5]** Refer to parts of stories, dramas, and poems when writing or speaking about a text, using terms such as chapter, scene, and stanza; describe how each successive part builds on earlier sections.
Every fable in the series begins and ends the same. It starts with Aesop's grandmother encouraging him to go find answers for himself and ends with her validating his conclusions. This gives the child a comforting frame of familiarity in which each story is told. As such, the child does not need to focus on the details of the beginning and end of each fable; they only need to focus on the main content. *The life lesson / moral is stated twice as an intrinsic part of each fable. The first time it is stated is by Aesop when he states the life lesson as something he has learned that day. The second time is when his grandmother validates the message.* *Stating the moral twice not only acts as a reinforcement technique but it also allows for secondary or alternative life lessons to be stated as well.*	
[RL.2.6] Acknowledge differences in the points of view of characters, including by speaking in a different voice for each character when reading dialogue aloud.	**[RL.3.6]** Distinguish their own point of view from that of the narrator or those of the characters.
The fable is told from Aesop's perspective. As such we know what he observes and also how he feels about events.	
Integration of Knowledge and Ideas	
[RL.2.7] Use information gained from the illustrations and words in a print to demonstrate understanding of its characters, setting, or plot.	**[RL.3.7]** Explain how specific aspects of a text's illustrations contribute to what is conveyed by the words in a story (e.g., create mood, emphasize aspects of a character or setting).
All illustrations of Nana are designed to convey love and support. The illustration of the bear over the boy is mimicked by the text that describes the seen and wraps around the bear: The big furry brown bear shuffled over to the boy and put his muzzle to the boy's ear. Sniff, sniff, sniff, went the bear as he stood over the frightened boy.	

The Friends and the Bear — Common Core Mapping — Reading Standards for Literature

[RL.2.9] Compare and contrast two or more versions of the same story (e.g., Cinderella stories) by different authors or from different cultures.	**[RL.3.9]** Compare and contrast the themes, settings, and plots of stories written by the same author about the same or similar characters (e.g., in books from a series).
Comparison with a classic adaptation: http://www.kids-pages.com/folders/stories/Aesops_Fables/page4.htm **Differences**: • The title of the classic story is 'The Bear and the Two Travelers' as opposed to the 'The Friends and the Bear' • Aesop is a character in the Aesop's Childhood Adventures (ACA) series while Aesop is not a character in the classic adaptation. • Story told from the perspective of Aesop as opposed to a narrator. • The moral of the classic story is: *Misfortune reveals the true nature of friends,* while the moral of ACA version is more explicit, defining friendship as someone who is there when you need them. **Similarities**: • The sequence of events are the same.	See #5 above, each story begins and ends the same. The theme of perseverance is an intrinsic part of every story and is illustrated by Aesop as he continues, every day to find the answers to his questions. The author believes that perseverance is a fundamental to success in life and is applicable in every conceivable area of life.

Aesop's 1st Book of Childhood Adventures — Teacher's Guide

The Friends and the Bear | Common Core Mapping | Reading Standards for Informational Text

Grade 2	Grade 3
Key Ideas and details	
[RI.2.1] Ask and answer such questions as who, what, where, when, why, and how to demonstrate understanding of key details in a text.	**[RI.3.1]** Ask and answer questions to demonstrate understanding of a text, referring explicitly to the text as the basis for the answers.

Who:
   Nana (f): Aesop's Grandmother.
   Aesop or Little Aesop (m): Protagonist. A young boy raccoon in the why stage of life who experience the fable as it unfolds.
   Taller boy (m): Teased the shorter boy, hid up in the tree and did not help the shorter boy.
   Shorter boy (m): To short to climb up in the tree, played dead and was almost eaten by the bear.
   Bear (m): Bear that frightened the boys, sniffed the shorter boy and almost ate him.
What: Frightening event causes Aesop to learn about the characteristics of good friendship.
Where: Deep in the forest behind his grandmother's cottage.
Why: The taller boy did not demonstrate true friendship.
How: Taller boy did not help the shorter boy when he needed him most.

[RI.2.2] Identify the main topic of a multi-paragraph text as well as the focus of specific paragraphs within the text.	**[RI.3.2]** Determine the main idea of a text; recount the key details and explain how they support the main idea.

True friendship illustrated via a frightening event where one boy abandons his 'friend'. Here are relevant excerpts from the story.
- *"Aesop, I don't know the answer to every question. Sometimes, you have to go and find the answer for yourself."*
- *"I will, Nana. Today is the day I will find out why."*
- *He (Aesop) poked his head around a bush and saw two boys walking toward him.*
- *The taller boy … was teasing the shorter boy who could not reach the leaves.*
- *A big, scary, brown bear rushed out from the forest … in front of the boys.*
- *Aesop was frightened for the boys, and yelled to them to play dead…*
- *The tall boy quickly grabbed a branch and pulled himself up, into the nearest tree.*
- *The shorter boy reached up to his friend and cried, "Pull me up! Pull me up!" His friend ignored him and instead climbed higher and higher …*
- *The shorter boy … threw himself down, … and pretended to be dead.*
- *The bear circled around the boy and put his muzzle to the boy's other ear. Sniff, sniff, sniff, .. and then with a low growl, walked back into the woods.*

	- … the taller boy jumped down from the tree, … and said, …"What did the bear whisper to you?" - The shorter boy … said, "He told me to never trust a friend who runs away when you need them most." - Little Aesop waited for the boys to leave and then he climbed down the tree to go home and tell his Nana about perseverance. - … he climbed into his grandmother's lap, "I still do not know why, but I did learn that a friend will always be there when you need them." - "I know you did not find what you were looking for, but you did learn about true friendship… a friend is your friend till the end." - "Don't worry about your questions, Aesop. Eventually, you will find the answers to all of them because you have perseverance."

Craft and Structure

[RI.2.4] Determine the meaning of words and phrases in a text relevant to a grade 2 topic or subject area.	**[RI.3.4]** Determine the meaning of general academic and domain-specific words and phrases in a text relevant to a grade 3 topic or subject area.

Each vocabulary word has no more than 3 definitions where the 1st is the preferred.

adventure
1. an exciting or very unusual experience
2. a bold, usually risky undertaking; hazardous action of uncertain outcome

cottage
1. a small house, usually of only one story.
2. a small, modest house at a lake, mountain resort, etc., owned or rented as a vacation home.

fable
1. a short tale to teach a moral lesson, often with animals or inanimate objects as characters
2. a story not founded on fact
3. legends or myths collectively

friendship
1. a person attached to another by feelings of affection or personal regard.
2. a person who gives assistance; patron; supporter

generations
1. the term of years, roughly 30 among human beings, accepted as the average period between the birth of parents and the birth of their offspring
2. a group of individuals, most of whom are the same approximate age, having similar ideas, problems, attitudes, etc.
3. a single step in natural descent, as of human beings, animals, or plants

The Friends and the Bear — Common Core Mapping — Reading Standards for Informational Text

generations
1. the term of years, roughly 30 among human beings, accepted as the average period between the birth of parents and the birth of their offspring
2. a group of individuals, most of whom are the same approximate age, having similar ideas, problems, attitudes, etc.
3. a single step in natural descent, as of human beings, animals, or plants

muzzle
1. the projecting part of the head of an animal, including jaws, mouth, and nose.
2. a device, usually an arrangement of straps, placed over an animal's mouth to prevent the animal from biting, eating, etc.
3. the mouth, or end for discharge, of the barrel of a gun, pistol, etc.

perseverance
1. steady persistence in a course of action or purpose, especially in spite of difficulties, obstacles, or discouragement

rustling noise
1. to move with a swishing or soft crackling sound such as that made by dry leaves rubbing together, or cause something to make such a sound
2. steal livestock: to steal livestock, especially cattle or horses

sparkle
1. to shine or glisten with little gleams of light, as a brilliant gem; glitter
2. to emit little sparks, as burning matter
3. to be brilliant, lively, or vivacious

[RI.2.5] Know and use various text features (e.g., captions, bold print, subheadings, glossaries, indexes, electronic menus, icons) to locate key facts or information in a text efficiently.	[RI.3.5] Use text features and search tools (e.g., key words, sidebars, hyperlinks) to locate information relevant to a given topic efficiently.
• *Sniff, sniff, sniff,* went the bear as he stood over the frightened boy. • *Sniff, sniff, sniff,* went the bear.	`n/a

Aesop's 1st Book of Childhood Adventures   Teacher's Guide

The Friends and the Bear   Common Core Mapping   Reading Standards for Informational Text

[RI.2.6] Identify the main purpose of a text, including what the author wants to answer, explain, or describe.	[RI.3.6] Distinguish their own point of view from that of the author of a text.
Lessons: • Never trust a friend who runs away when you need them most. –> Fact: The taller boy hid when the shorter boy asked for help. • A good friend will always be there when you need them. –> Fact: The taller boy ignored the shorter boy asked for help. • A friend is your friend till the end. –> Fact: The taller boy was not by the shorter boy's side. Spelling Tip: A fri**end** is your fri**end** till the **end**.	Applicable but requires student input.

Integration of Knowledge and Ideas

[RI.2.7] Explain how specific images (e.g., a diagram showing how a machine works) contribute to and clarify a text.	[RI.3.7] Use information gained from illustrations (e.g., maps, photographs) and the words in a text to demonstrate understanding of the text (e.g., where, when, why, and how key events occur).
Option 1: Have each student draw the racetrack based on the description in the story then compare and contrast them. Description: *When the mouse returned he stood by the tree and said, "The race will start here. You will run past the big boulder, and go down the hill. Then you will run around the clover field and back up the hill to this tree. The first one to the finish line wins the race."* Option 2: Point out how the illustration of a clover provides sufficient information to imagine the clover field. Also the lady bug provides a rough size comparison.	

[RI.2.9] Compare and contrast the most important points presented by two texts on the same topic.	[RI.3.9] Compare and contrast the most important points and key details presented in two texts on the same topic.
Comparison with a classic adaptation: http://www.kids-pages.com/folders/stories/Aesops_Fables/page4.htm **Differences**: • The title of the classic story is 'The Bear and the Two Travelers' as opposed to the 'The Friends and the Bear' • Aesop is a character in the Aesop's Childhood Adventures (ACA) series while Aesop is not a character in the classic adaptation. • Story told from the perspective of Aesop as opposed to a narrator. • The moral of the classic story is: *Misfortune reveals the true nature of friends,* while the moral of ACA version is more explicit, defining friendship as someone who is there when you need them. **Similarities**: • The sequence of events are the same.	

The Friends and the Bear — Common Core Mapping — Writing

Grade 1	Grade 2
Text Types and Purposes	

Grade 1	Grade 2
[W.1.1] Write opinion pieces in which they introduce the topic or name the book they are writing about, state an opinion, supply a reason for the opinion, and provide some sense of closure.	**[W.2.1]** Write opinion pieces in which they introduce the topic or book they are writing about, state an opinion, supply reasons that support the opinion, use linking words (e.g., *because*, *and*, *also*) to connect opinion and reasons, and provide a concluding statement or section.

Ask the children to think about who their favorite character is and why. Then ask them to write down the name of the story; who their favorite character is; and why that character is their favorite.

Characters:
- Nana (f): Aesop's Grandmother.
- Aesop or Little Aesop (m): Protagonist. A young boy raccoon in the why stage of life who experience the fable as it unfolds.
- Taller boy (m): Teased the shorter boy, hid up in the tree and did not help the shorter boy.
- Shorter boy (m): To short to climb up in the tree, played dead and was almost eaten by the bear.
- Bear (m): Bear that frightened the boys, sniffed the shorter boy and almost ate him.

Grade 1	Grade 2
[W.1.2] Write informative/explanatory texts in which they name a topic, supply some facts about the topic, and provide some sense of closure.	**[W.2.2]** Write informative/explanatory texts in which they introduce a topic, use facts and definitions to develop points, and provide a concluding statement or section.

Ask the children to think about the lesson(s) they learned from the story and why it is important lesson. Then have them write about it.

Lessons:
- Never trust a friend who runs away when you need them most. –> Fact: The taller boy hid when the shorter boy asked for help.
- A good friend will always be there when you need them. –> Fact: The taller boy ignored the shorter boy asked for help.
- A friend is your friend till the end. –> Fact: The taller boy was not by the shorter boy's side.
  Spelling Tip: A fri<u>end</u> is your fri<u>end</u> till the **end**.

The Friends and the Bear — Common Core Mapping — **Writing**

[W.1.3] Write narratives in which they recount two or more appropriately sequenced events, include some details regarding what happened, use temporal words to signal event order, and provide some sense of closure.	**[W.2.3]** Write narratives in which they recount a well-elaborated event or short sequence of events, include details to describe actions, thoughts, and feelings, use temporal words to signal event order, and provide a sense of closure.
Aesop went out searching for an answer to his question. He happened upon 2 boys walking in the forest. They were pulling at the leaves on branches. A bear came out of the woods and the taller boy climbed up into the tree to hide. The shorter boy reached up for help but the taller boy ignored him. The shorter boy played dead. The bear came over to the boy and sniffed to see if he was really dead then walked away. The taller boy asked what the bear said and the shorter boy answered – 'never trust a friend who runs away when you need him most.' Aesop then returned to Nana's house and told her what happened.	See grade 1 and: Nana: Without her encouragement, Aesop would not have gone out and seen the 2 boys and the bear. Aesop: Was shy so he hid from the boys. He was worried that the bear would hurt the boys and was frustrated that he could not tell the shorter boy to play dead. Aesop was also frightened for his own safety. Taller boy: Teased the shorter boy because he could not reach the leaves. Shorter boy: Was shaking with fear because of the bear.
Production and Distribution of Writing	
[W.1.5] With guidance and support from adults, focus on a topic, respond to questions and suggestions from peers, and add details to strengthen writing as needed.	**[W.2.5]** With guidance and support from adults and peers, focus on a topic and strengthen writing as needed by revising and editing.
Teacher directed.	Teacher directed.
[W.1.6] With guidance and support from adults, use a variety of digital tools to produce and publish writing, including in collaboration with peers.	**[W.2.6]** With guidance and support from adults, use a variety of digital tools to produce and publish writing, including in collaboration with peers.
Teacher directed.	Teacher directed.
Research to Build and Present Knowledge	
[W.1.8] With guidance and support from adults, recall information from experiences or gather information from provided sources to answer a question.	**[W.2.8]** Recall information from experiences or gather information from provided sources to answer a question.
Have you ever been a good friend or do you know someone who is?	Describe why.

The Friends and the Bear   Common Core Mapping   Writing

Grade 3	Grade 4
Text Types and Purposes	
[W.3.1] Write opinion pieces on topics or texts, supporting a point of view with reasons. • **[W.3.1a]** Introduce the topic or text they are writing about, state an opinion, and create an organizational structure that lists reasons. • **[W.3.1b]** Provide reasons that support the opinion. • **[W.3.1c]** Use linking words and phrases (e.g., *because, therefore, since, for example*) to connect opinion and reasons. • **[W.3.1d]** Provide a concluding statement or section.	**[W.4.1]** Write opinion pieces on topics or texts, supporting a point of view with reasons and information. • **W.4.1a]** Introduce a topic or text clearly, state an opinion, and create an organizational structure in which related ideas are grouped to support the writer's purpose. • **[W.4.1b]** Provide reasons that are supported by facts and details. • **[W.4.1c]** Link opinion and reasons using words and phrases (e.g., f*or instance, in order to, in addition*). • **[W.4.1d]** Provide a concluding statement or section related to the opinion presented.

Option 1:
• Ask the children if the taller boy should have helped his friend, or if the taller boy should have stayed on the ground with his friend, or do what he did. Then ask them to write an opinion piece as described above.
 	
Option 2:
Ask the children to think about who their favorite character is and why. Then ask them to write an opinion piece as described above.
Characters:
   Nana (f): Aesop's Grandmother.
   Aesop or Little Aesop (m): Protagonist. A young boy raccoon in the why stage of life who experience the fable as it unfolds.
   Taller boy (m): Teased the shorter boy, hid up in the tree and did not help the shorter boy.
   Shorter boy (m): To short to climb up in the tree, played dead and was almost eaten by the bear.
   Bear (m): Bear that frightened the boys and sniffed the shorter boy.	

The Crow and the Pitcher

Common Core
Mapping

The Crow and the Pitcher

"But why Nana, why?" asked Aesop.

With a big smile and a sparkle in her eye, the older one said, "Aesop, I don't know the answer to every question. Sometimes, you have to go and find the answer for yourself."

"I will, Nana. Today is the day I will find out why."

Little Aesop looked up at his grandmother. He jumped

out of her lap and on to the floor. He ran through the den, down the hall and out the door.

It was a beautiful sunny day; perfect weather for Little Aesop to go out and play.

Soon, Little Aesop came upon a picnic table that had a pitcher on it. He noticed that the pitcher was half full of water.

Aesop turned to continue on his way when his friend the crow came swooping down and landed next to him.

"Hi," said Aesop. "How are you? It has been a long time since I last saw you."

"Hi Aesop," whispered the crow. "I am so thirsty that I can barely talk. Do you know where I can get some water?"

"Yup, from the pitcher on the picnic table."

The bird hopped up onto the pitcher and tried to drink the water, but he could not reach it. He tried and he tried, but the water was simply not high enough.

Aesop could see that his friend was very thirsty. He wanted to help him, but he did not know how.

Aesop watched as the crow strutted back and forth looking into the pitcher and then looking all around. The bird was very thirsty and very frustrated.

All of a sudden, the crow stopped strutting. He jumped off the picnic table and picked up a pebble.

"No! Stop! Don't eat that pebble!" yelled Aesop.

"Eat the pebble? I am not going to do that!" said the crow. "I am going to drop the pebble into the pitcher."

"What? Why?" asked Aesop.

"So I can drink the water. I think I can solve this problem."

"Oh boy, now I'm really confused," said Aesop.

The crow flew up onto the table, dropped the pebble into the pitcher and said, "Watch this."

Aesop was still very confused.

The bird spied another pebble, flew down and grabbed it.

He dropped that pebble into the pitcher. He then found another, and another.

The crow turned toward Aesop and said, "Look at the water in the pitcher. It has moved up a little bit hasn't it?"

"It has! I don't believe it," said Aesop. "But it is not high enough for you to drink yet. What are you going to do?"

"That is OK," said the crow. "With a little hard work, I will collect enough pebbles to get a drink. Will you help me collect pebbles?"

"I sure will," said Aesop. He was happy that there was something he could do to help his friend.

Aesop and the crow continued gathering pebbles and dropping them into the pitcher.

After a while the water rose high enough for the crow to get a drink.

When the crow was

finished drinking, he said, "That was the best drink of water I have ever had."

"I'll bet it was," said Aesop.

The crow then stretched his wings and gave a big yawn. "It is time for me to get back to my nest, Aesop. Good bye, and thanks for all of your help."

"You're welcome," said Aesop as he headed home.

"I'm happy to see you my little one," said Aesop's grandmother, who was sitting in the den. "Did you find what you were looking for? Did you get the answer to your questions?"

"No," said Aesop as he climbed into his grandmother's lap, "I still do not know why,

but I did learn that most problems can be fixed with a good idea and a little hard work."

"That is very good Aesop; tell me more."

"Well, I saw my friend, Crow, today. He was very thirsty…"

When Aesop was finished telling his grandmother everything that happened, she looked at the young one with a big smile and a sparkle in her eye and said, "It sounds like you had a great adventure today. I know you did not find what you were looking for, but you did learn the importance of thinking about a problem and working hard to solve it."

She then hugged Aesop and said, "Don't worry about your questions, Aesop. Eventually, you will find the answers to all of them because you have perseverance."

The Crow and the Pitcher   Common Core Mapping   Reading Standards for Literature

Grade 2	Grade 3
Key Ideas and details	
[RL.2.1] Ask and answer such questions as who, what, where, when, why, and how to demonstrate understanding of key details in a text.	**[RL.3.1]** Ask and answer questions to demonstrate understanding of a text, referring explicitly to the text as the basis for the answers.
Who: Nana (f): Aesop's Grandmother Aesop or Little Aesop (m): Protagonist Crow (m): Aesop's friend who was very thirsty and figured out how to get himself a drink. **What:** Pitcher of water **Where:** Picnic table, neighborhood. **Why:** To get a drink of water to quench Crow's thirst. **How:** Displaced water in the pitcher with pebbles causing the water level to rise. Thinking about the problem and working diligently to completion. The crow exemplified ingenuity, a good work ethic, and perseverance.	
[RL.2.2] Recount stories, including fables and folktales from diverse cultures, and determine their central message, lesson, or moral.	**[RL.3.2]** Recount stories, including fables, folktales, and myths from diverse cultures; determine the central message, lesson, or moral and explain how it is conveyed through key details in the text.
Lessons: Most problems can be fixed with a good idea and a little hard work. The importance of completing a task.	

The Crow and the Pitcher — Common Core Mapping — Reading Standards for Literature

[RL.2.3] Describe how characters in a story respond to major events and challenges.	[RL.3.3] Describe characters in a story (e.g., their traits, motivations, or feelings) and explain how their actions contribute to the sequence of events.
Nana: Encouraged Aesop to find answers and validated his conclusions upon return. Aesop: Went out to find answers to his questions. He happened upon his friend Crow and encouraged him to drink the water in the pitcher. Then he helped his friend find pebbles. Crow: Was unable to reach the water in the pitcher so he dropped pebbles into the pitcher to displace the water and cause the water level to rise.	See grade 2 and: Nana: Without her encouragement, Aesop would not have gone out and found his friend Crow. Aesop: Was worried that Crow would be ill because he was so thirsty. He encouraged his friend to find a solution and helped him complete the task (collecting pebbles) that solved the problem. Crow: Motivated by thirst to find a way to reach the water in the pitcher. He was also confident in his ability to solve the problem.

Craft and Structure

[RL.2.4] Describe how words and phrases (e.g., regular beats, alliteration, rhymes, repeated lines) supply rhythm and meaning in a story, poem, or song.	[RL.3.4] Determine the meaning of words and phrases as they are used in a text, distinguishing literal from non-literal language.
The following illustrates happiness & excitement through rhythm and speed: - Little Aesop looked up at his grandmother. He jumped out of her lap and on to the floor. He ran through the den, down the hall and out the door. - It was a beautiful sunny day, perfect weather for Little Aesop to go out and play. - "… a friend is your friend till the end."	Non-literal: "When the crow was finished drinking, he said, "That was the best drink of water I have ever had." Literal: "Hi Aesop," whispered the crow. "I am so thirsty that I can barely talk."

The Crow and the Pitcher   Common Core Mapping   Reading Standards for Literature

[RL.2.5] Describe the overall structure of a story, including describing how the beginning introduces the story and the ending concludes the action.	**[RL.3.5]** Refer to parts of stories, dramas, and poems when writing or speaking about a text, using terms such as chapter, scene, and stanza; describe how each successive part builds on earlier sections.
colspan Every fable in the series begins and ends the same. It starts with Aesop's grandmother encouraging him to go find answers for himself and ends with her validating his conclusions. This gives the child a comforting frame of familiarity in which each story is told. As such, the child does not need to focus on the details of the beginning and end of each fable; they only need to focus on the main content. The life lesson / moral is stated twice as an intrinsic part of each fable. The first time it is stated is by Aesop when he states the life lesson as something he has learned that day. The second time is when his grandmother validates the message. Stating the moral twice not only acts as a reinforcement technique but it also allows for secondary or alternative life lessons to be stated as well.	
[RL.2.6] Acknowledge differences in the points of view of characters, including by speaking in a different voice for each character when reading dialogue aloud.	**[RL.3.6]** Distinguish their own point of view from that of the narrator or those of the characters.
The fable is told from Aesop's perspective. As such we know what he observes and also how he feels about events.	
Integration of Knowledge and Ideas	
[RL.2.7] Use information gained from the illustrations and words in a print to demonstrate understanding of its characters, setting, or plot.	**[RL.3.7]** Explain how specific aspects of a text's illustrations contribute to what is conveyed by the words in a story (e.g., create mood, emphasize aspects of a character or setting).
All illustrations of Nana are designed to convey love and support. All of the animals are black and white so that the child can fill in the colors with their imagination.	

The Crow and the Pitcher — Common Core Mapping — Reading Standards for Literature

[RL.2.9] Compare and contrast two or more versions of the same story (e.g., Cinderella stories) by different authors or from different cultures.	[RL.3.9] Compare and contrast the themes, settings, and plots of stories written by the same author about the same or similar characters (e.g., in books from a series).

Comparison with a classic adaptation: http://www.americanliterature.com/author/aesop/short-story/the-crow-and-the-pitcher
Differences:
• Aesop is a character in the Aesop's Childhood Adventures (ACA) series while Aesop is not a character in the classic adaptation.
• Story told from the perspective of Aesop as opposed to a narrator.
• The feels and concerns of the crow are described in ACA
• There are two morals in ACA.
• The moral of working hard to solve a problem is not identified in the classic adaptation but is in ACA.
• Only one illustration in the classic adaptation.
• The classic adaptation declares the life lesson as "Necessity is the mother of invention" while ACA weaves the meaning of the life lesson into the story as:
   - Most problems can be fixed with a good idea and a little hard work.
   - The importance of completing a task and not giving up or being overwhelmed by a problem i.e. perseverance.
Similarities:
• The basic story and life lesson are the same.
• Necessity is the mother of invention is described in both (in different terms).
	See #5 above, each story begins and ends the same.
	
	The theme of perseverance is an intrinsic part of every story and is illustrated by Aesop as he continues, every day to find the answers to his questions. The author believes that perseverance is a fundamental to success in life and is applicable in every conceivable area of life.

The Crow and the Pitcher — Common Core Mapping — Reading Standards for Informational Text

Grade 2	Grade 3
Key Ideas and details	
[RI.2.1] Ask and answer such questions as who, what, where, when, why, and how to demonstrate understanding of key details in a text.	**[RI.3.1]** Ask and answer questions to demonstrate understanding of a text, referring explicitly to the text as the basis for the answers.

Who:
   Nana (f): Aesop's Grandmother
   Aesop or Little Aesop (m): Protagonist
   Crow (m): Aesop's friend who was very thirsty and figured out how to get himself a drink.
What: Pitcher of water
Where: Picnic table, neighborhood.
Why: To get a drink of water to quench Crow's thirst.
How: Displaced water in the pitcher with pebbles causing the water level to rise. Thinking about the problem and working diligently to completion. The crow exemplified ingenuity, a good work ethic, and perseverance.	

[RI.2.2] Identify the main topic of a multi-paragraph text as well as the focus of specific paragraphs within the text.	**[RI.3.2]** Determine the main idea of a text; recount the key details and explain how they support the main idea.
Necessity is the mother of invention. Ingenuity. Not giving up and finding a solution. People like to help others in need and enjoy their success. Here are relevant excerpts from the story. • … Aesop came upon a picnic table that had a pitcher on it. He noticed that the pitcher was half full of water. • "I (Crow) am so thirsty that I can barely talk. Do you know where I can get some water?" • The bird hopped up onto the pitcher and tried to drink the water, but he could not reach it. • He (Aesop) wanted to help him (crow), but he did not know how. • All of a sudden, the crow stopped strutting. He jumped off the picnic table and picked up a pebble. • "I (Crow) am going to drop the pebble into the pitcher." … "So I can drink the water. I think I can solve this problem." • "But it is not high enough for you to drink yet. What are you going to do?" "That is OK," said the crow. "With a little hard work, I will collect enough pebbles to get a drink. • He (Aesop) was happy that there was something he could do to help his friend. • After a while the water rose high enough for the crow to get a drink. • "I still do not know why, but I did learn that most problems can be fixed with a good idea and a little hard work." • … but you did learn the importance of thinking about a problem and working hard to solve it." "I know you did not find what you were looking for, but you did learn that bragging can hurt people and anything is possible with perseverance." • "Don't worry about your questions, Aesop. Eventually, you will find the answers to all of them because you have perseverance."	

The Crow and the Pitcher — Common Core Mapping — Reading Standards for Informational Text

[RI.2.3] Describe the connection between a series of historical events, scientific ideas or concepts, or steps in technical procedures in a text.	[RI.3.3] Describe the relationship between a series of historical events, scientific ideas or concepts, or steps in technical procedures in a text, using language that pertains to time, sequence, and cause/effect.

- *He jumped off the picnic table and picked up a pebble.*
- *"I am going to drop the pebble into the pitcher."*
- *The crow flew up onto the table, dropped the pebble into the pitcher and said, "Watch this."*
- *The bird spied another pebble, flew down and grabbed it. He dropped that pebble into the pitcher. He then found another, and another.*
- *The crow turned toward Aesop and said, "Look at the water in the pitcher. It has moved up a little bit hasn't it?"*
- *"It has! I don't believe it," said Aesop. "But it is not high enough for you to drink yet. What are you going to do?"*
- *"That is OK," said the crow. "With a little hard work, I will collect enough pebbles to get a drink. Will you help me collect pebbles?"*
- *Aesop and the crow continued gathering pebbles and dropping them into the pitcher. After a while the water rose high enough for the crow to get a drink.*

Craft and Structure

[RI.2.4] Determine the meaning of words and phrases in a text relevant to a grade 2 topic or subject area.	[RI.3.4] Determine the meaning of general academic and domain-specific words and phrases in a text relevant to a grade 3 topic or subject area.

Each vocabulary word has no more than 3 definitions where the 1st is the preferred.

adventure
1. an exciting or very unusual experience
2. a bold, usually risky undertaking; hazardous action of uncertain outcome

crow
1. any of several large oscine birds of the genus Corvus, of the family Corvidae, having a long, stout bill, lustrous black plumage, and a wedge-shaped tail.
2. to gloat or boast

fable
1. a short tale to teach a moral lesson, often with animals or inanimate objects as characters
2. a story not founded on fact
3. legends or myths collectively

frustrated
1. dissatisfaction: a feeling of disappointment, exasperation, or weariness caused by goals being thwarted or desires unsatisfied
2. having a feeling of or filled with dissatisfaction resulting from unfulfilled needs or unresolved problems.

The Crow and the Pitcher Common Core Mapping Reading Standards for Informational Text

generations
1. the term of years, roughly 30 among human beings, accepted as the average period between the birth of parents and the birth of their offspring
2. a group of individuals, most of whom are the same approximate age, having similar ideas, problems, attitudes, etc.
3. a single step in natural descent, as of human beings, animals, or plants

perseverance
1. steady persistence in a course of action or purpose, especially in spite of difficulties, obstacles, or discouragement

pitcher
1. a container, usually with a handle and spout or lip, for holding and pouring liquids.
2. a person who throws the ball to the opposing batter.

solve this problem
1. to shine or glisten with little gleams of light, as a brilliant gem; glitter
2. to emit little sparks, as burning matter

sparkle
1. to shine or glisten with little gleams of light, as a brilliant gem; glitter
2. to emit little sparks, as burning matter
3. to be brilliant, lively, or vivacious

spied
1. to search or look for closely or carefully.
2. to observe secretively or furtively with hostile intent

strutted
1. to walk with determined intent.
2. to walk with a vain, pompous bearing, as with head erect and chest thrown out, as if expecting to impress observers.

swooping
1. to come down from the air upon something.
2. to sweep through the air, as a bird or a bat, especially down upon prey.
3. to take, lift, scoop up, or remove with or as with one sweeping motion

The Crow and the Pitcher — Common Core Mapping — Reading Standards for Informational Text

[RI.2.6] Identify the main purpose of a text, including what the author wants to answer, explain, or describe.	**[RI.3.6]** Distinguish their own point of view from that of the author of a text.
Lessons: Most problems can be fixed with a good idea and a little hard work. The importance of completing a task and not giving up or being overwhelmed by a problem i.e. perseverance.	Applicable but requires student input.

Integration of Knowledge and Ideas

[RI.2.7] Explain how specific images (e.g., a diagram showing how a machine works) contribute to and clarify a text.	**[RI.3.7]** Use information gained from illustrations (e.g., maps, photographs) and the words in a text to demonstrate understanding of the text (e.g., where, when, why, and how key events occur).

The illustrations on pages 31, 32 and 34 show the gradual rising of the water caused by the increased number of pebbles. The following text supports the illustrations.
"I am going to drop the pebble into the pitcher."
The crow flew up onto the table, dropped the pebble into the pitcher and said, "Watch this."
The bird spied another pebble, flew down and grabbed it. He dropped that pebble into the pitcher. He then found another, and another.
The crow turned toward Aesop and said, "Look at the water in the pitcher. It has moved up a little bit hasn't it?"
"It has! I don't believe it," said Aesop. "But it is not high enough for you to drink yet.
Aesop and the crow continued gathering pebbles and dropping them into the pitcher. After a while the water rose high enough for the crow to get a drink.

The Crow and the Pitcher — Common Core Mapping — Reading Standards for Informational Text

[RI.2.9] Compare and contrast the most important points presented by two texts on the same topic.	**[RI.3.9]** Compare and contrast the most important points and key details presented in two texts on the same topic.

Comparison with a classic adaptation: http://www.americanliterature.com/author/aesop/short-story/the-crow-and-the-pitcher

Differences:
• Aesop is a character in the Aesop's Childhood Adventures (ACA) series while Aesop is not a character in the classic adaptation.
• Story told from the perspective of Aesop as opposed to a narrator.
• The feels and concerns of the crow are described in ACA
• There are two morals in ACA.
• The moral of working hard to solve a problem is not identified in the classic adaptation but is in ACA.
• Only one illustration in the classic adaptation.
• The classic adaptation declares the life lesson as "Necessity is the mother of invention" while ACA weaves the meaning of the life lesson into the story as:
  - Most problems can be fixed with a good idea and a little hard work.
  - The importance of completing a task and not giving up or being overwhelmed by a problem i.e. perseverance.

Similarities:
• The basic story and life lesson are the same.
• Necessity is the mother of invention is described in both (in different terms).

The Crow and the Pitcher Common Core Mapping Writing

Grade 1	Grade 2
Text Types and Purposes	
[W.1.1] Write opinion pieces in which they introduce the topic or name the book they are writing about, state an opinion, supply a reason for the opinion, and provide some sense of closure.	**[W.2.1]** Write opinion pieces in which they introduce the topic or book they are writing about, state an opinion, supply reasons that support the opinion, use linking words (e.g., *because*, *and*, *also*) to connect opinion and reasons, and provide a concluding statement or section.

Ask the children to think about who their favorite character is and why. Then ask them to write down the name of the story; who their favorite character is; and why that character is their favorite. **Characters:**
  Nana (f): Aesop's Grandmother.
  Aesop or Little Aesop (m): Protagonist. A young boy raccoon in the why stage of life who experience the fable as it unfolds.
  Crow (m): Crow was very thirsty and was looking for some water. He found the water but could not get at it so he thought long and hard about it until he found a solution. Then he worked diligently until he was able to drink.	

[W.1.2] Write informative/explanatory texts in which they name a topic, supply some facts about the topic, and provide some sense of closure.	**[W.2.2]** Write informative/explanatory texts in which they introduce a topic, use facts and definitions to develop points, and provide a concluding statement or section.
Ask the children to think about the lesson(s) they learned from the story and why it is important lesson. Then have them write about it. **Lessons:** • Most problems can be fixed with a good idea. –> Fact: Initially, neither Aesop nor Crow had any idea how to solve the problem but eventually found a novel solution. • Most problems can be fixed with a little hard work. –> : The pitcher required lots of pebbles and kept both Aesop and Crow busy. • Perseverance. –> Fact: The crow strutted back and forth, thinking hard about the problem until he found a solution, then he gathered pebbles, one by one until he was finished	

The Crow and the Pitcher — Common Core Mapping — Writing

[W.1.3] Write narratives in which they recount two or more appropriately sequenced events, include some details regarding what happened, use temporal words to signal event order, and provide some sense of closure. Aesop went out searching for an answer to his question. He happened upon his friend Crow who was very thirsty. He also found a pitcher partially full of water but Crow could not get a drink. Crow found a solution and Aesop helped crow fill the pitcher with pebbles which in turn raised the water level so Crow could drink. He then returned to Nana's house and told her what happened.	**[W.2.3]** Write narratives in which they recount a well-elaborated event or short sequence of events, include details to describe actions, thoughts, and feelings, use temporal words to signal event order, and provide a sense of closure. See grade 1 and: Nana: Without her encouragement, Aesop would not have gone out and found his friend Crow. Aesop: Was happy to find his friend Crow. He wanted to help is friend and was upset that he did not know how. Eventually he did help him and was happy. Crow: Was very thirsty. He thought long and hard about the problem and devised a solution. He then asked his friend to help him and he kept at the task i.e. persevered until the task was finished. Finally, he enjoyed the best drink he had ever had..
**Production and Distribution of Writing**	
[W.1.5] With guidance and support from adults, focus on a topic, respond to questions and suggestions from peers, and add details to strengthen writing as needed. Teacher directed.	**[W.2.5]** With guidance and support from adults and peers, focus on a topic and strengthen writing as needed by revising and editing. Teacher directed.
[W.1.6] With guidance and support from adults, use a variety of digital tools to produce and publish writing, including in collaboration with peers. Teacher directed.	**[W.2.6]** With guidance and support from adults, use a variety of digital tools to produce and publish writing, including in collaboration with peers. Teacher directed.
Research to Build and Present Knowledge	
[W.1.8] With guidance and support from adults, recall information from experiences or gather information from provided sources to answer a question. Have you have ever had a very difficult problem and then found a great solution? Describe the problem. Describe the solution. Have you ever been frustrated or sad because you wanted to help but did not know how? Describe what happened. Have you ever put something in a container of water and caused it to over flow? Describe the container. Describe what happened. Have you ever been a good friend or do you know someone who is? Describe why.	**[W.2.8]** Recall information from experiences or gather information from provided sources to answer a question.

The Crow and the Pitcher — Common Core Mapping — Writing

Grade 3	Grade 4
Text Types and Purposes	
[W.3.1] Write opinion pieces on topics or texts, supporting a point of view with reasons. • **[W.3.1a]** Introduce the topic or text they are writing about, state an opinion, and create an organizational structure that lists reasons. • **[W.3.1b]** Provide reasons that support the opinion. • **[W.3.1c]** Use linking words and phrases (e.g., *because*, *therefore*, *since*, *for example*) to connect opinion and reasons. • **[W.3.1d]** Provide a concluding statement or section.	**[W.4.1]** Write opinion pieces on topics or texts, supporting a point of view with reasons and information. • **W.4.1a]** Introduce a topic or text clearly, state an opinion, and create an organizational structure in which related ideas are grouped to support the writer's purpose. • **[W.4.1b]** Provide reasons that are supported by facts and details. • **[W.4.1c]** Link opinion and reasons using words and phrases (e.g., *for instance*, *in order to*, *in addition*). • **[W.4.1d]** Provide a concluding statement or section related to the opinion presented.

Option 1:
- Ask the children if all problems can be solved with a good idea and hard work? Then ask them to write an opinion piece as described above.

Option 2:
Ask the children to think about who their favorite character is and why. Then ask them to write an opinion piece as described above.
Characters:
Nana (f): Aesop's Grandmother
Aesop or Little Aesop (m): Protagonist
Crow (m): Aesop's friend who was very thirsty and figured out how to get himself a drink.

Common Core ELA Worksheets
for

The Crow and the Pitcher

Aesop's
1st Book of
Childhood Adventures

http://www.aesopsadventures.com/

Aesop's 1st Book of Childhood Adventures

Character Traits

Teacher's Guide

Who

Name: _____ **Date:** _____

Aesop's 1st Book of Childhood Adventures

Teacher's Guide

Who are the characters?

Name   **Who**   **Where**

Name	Who	Where
	A nice raccoon boy who went on an adventure to find the answer to his question.	Near his Nana's cottage.
		Warm cosy cottage.

Name: _____ Date: _____

Common Core Standard: RL.2.1, RL.3.1, RI.2.1, RI.3.1

98

Copyright 2013 by Vangelo Media

Aesop's 1st Book of Childhood Adventures   Teacher's Guide

Story Facts

What?	

Where?	

When?	

Why?	

How?	

Name: _____   Date: _____

Common Core Standard: RL.2.1, RL.3.1, RI.2.1, RI.3.1, W.1.2, W.2.2

Aesop's 1st Book of Childhood Adventures

Teacher's Guide

Moral Lessons Learned

Fables are stories that teach a lesson about life. Some fables have more than one life lesson or moral.

Lesson #1:

Lesson #2:

Name: _____ Date: _____

Who did this?

Connect these

Crow ○

Nana ○

Aesop ○

○ Told Aesop to find answers to his questions and discussed what he learned.

○ Went out to find answers to his questions.

○ Did not give up until he figured out how to get a drink.

○ Worked very hard gathering and dropping pebbles into a pitcher to make the water level rise.

○ Wanted to help his friend.

Pick one of the characters and describe what you liked or disliked about what they did.

Name: _____ Date: _____

Aesop's 1st Book of Childhood Adventures

Teacher's Guide

What does this mean?

"I am so thirsty that I can barely talk."

Literal ☐   Non-literal ☐

Describe what this means:

"The hare took off like a dart."

Literal ☐   Non-literal ☐

Describe what this means:

Name: _____   **Date:** _____

Aesop's 1st Book of Childhood Adventures

Story Sequencing

Teacher's Guide

Topic: _____

Name: _____   Date: _____

Common Core Standard: RI.2.3, RI.3.3, W.1.1, W2.1

Aesop's 1st Book of Childhood Adventures — Teacher's Guide

Story Structure

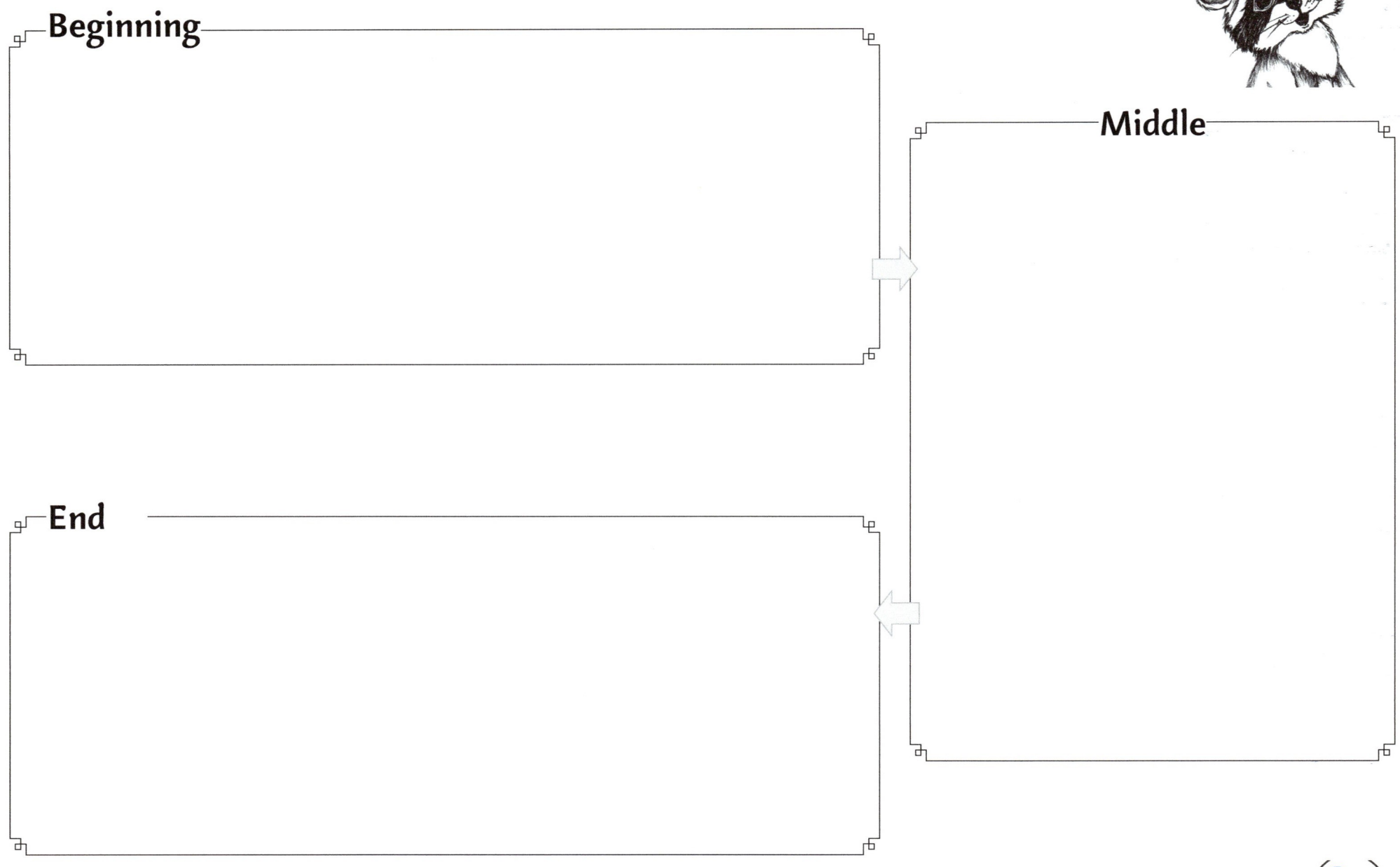

Beginning

Middle

End

Name: _____ **Date:** _____

Common Core Std: RI.2.5

Aesop's 1st Book of Childhood Adventures — Teacher's Guide

Who said... ?

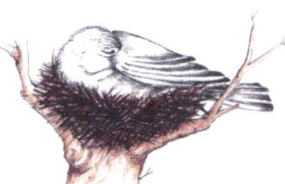

"No! Stop! Don't eat that pebble!" yelled _____.

Was the crow going to eat the pebble? Why?

Would you eat a pebble if you were thirsty? Why?

"Oh boy, now I'm really confused," said _____.

Why is he confused?

Were you confused? Why?

Name: _____ **Date:** _____

Aesop's 1st Book of Childhood Adventures

Vocabulary
(page 1 of 2)

Teacher's Guide

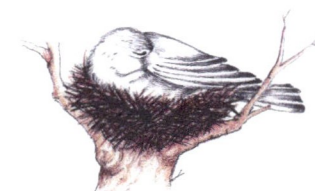

adventure
An exciting or very unusual experience.
"It sounds like you had a great adventure today..."

crow
A large, black songbird.
Aesop watched as the crow strutted back and forth looking into the pitcher and then looking all around.

fable
A short tale to teach a moral lesson, often with animals.
Aesop's Fables

frustrated
Disappointed, thwarted and unsatisfied.
The bird was very thirsty and very frustrated.

generations
All the people born about the same time.
To my family, who taught me the importance of life lessons and the value of passing them on to future generations.

perseverance
To work steadily toward a goal while overcoming difficulties.
"Don't worry about your questions, Aesop. Eventually, you will find the answers to all of them because you have perseverance."

pitcher
A container, with a handle and a spout, for holding and pouring liquids.
"Yup, from the pitcher on the picnic table."

solve
To find a solution to a problem or puzzle.
"So I can drink the water. I think I can solve this problem."

Name: _____ Date: _____

Vocabulary
(page 2 of 2)

sparkle
To shine, glitter or glisten with little.
With a big smile and a sparkle in her eye, the older one said, "Aesop, I don't know the answer to every question...

spied
To carefully search or look for something.
The bird spied another pebble, flew down and grabbed it.

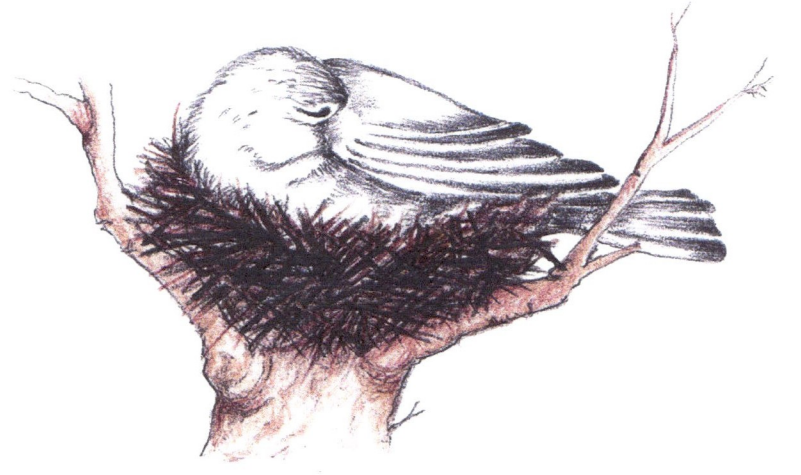

strutted
To walk with determination and purpose.
Aesop watched as the crow strutted back and forth looking into the pitcher and then looking all around.

swooping
To come down, sweeping through the air, upon something.
Aesop turned to continue on his way when his friend Crow came swooping down and landed next to him.

Name: _____ Date: _____

Do you agree?

With a little hard work you can solve almost any problem.

Do you agree? _____ Why?

"That the best drink of water I ever had," said the crow.

Do you agree? _____ Why?

Name: _____ Date: _____

Do you agree? Why?

With a little hard work you can solve almost any problem.

Name: _____ Date: _____

Do you agree? Why?

"That the best drink of water I ever had," said the crow.

Name: _____ Date: _____

www.ingramcontent.com/pod-product-compliance
Lightning Source LLC
Chambersburg PA
CBHW060813010526
44117CB00002B/21